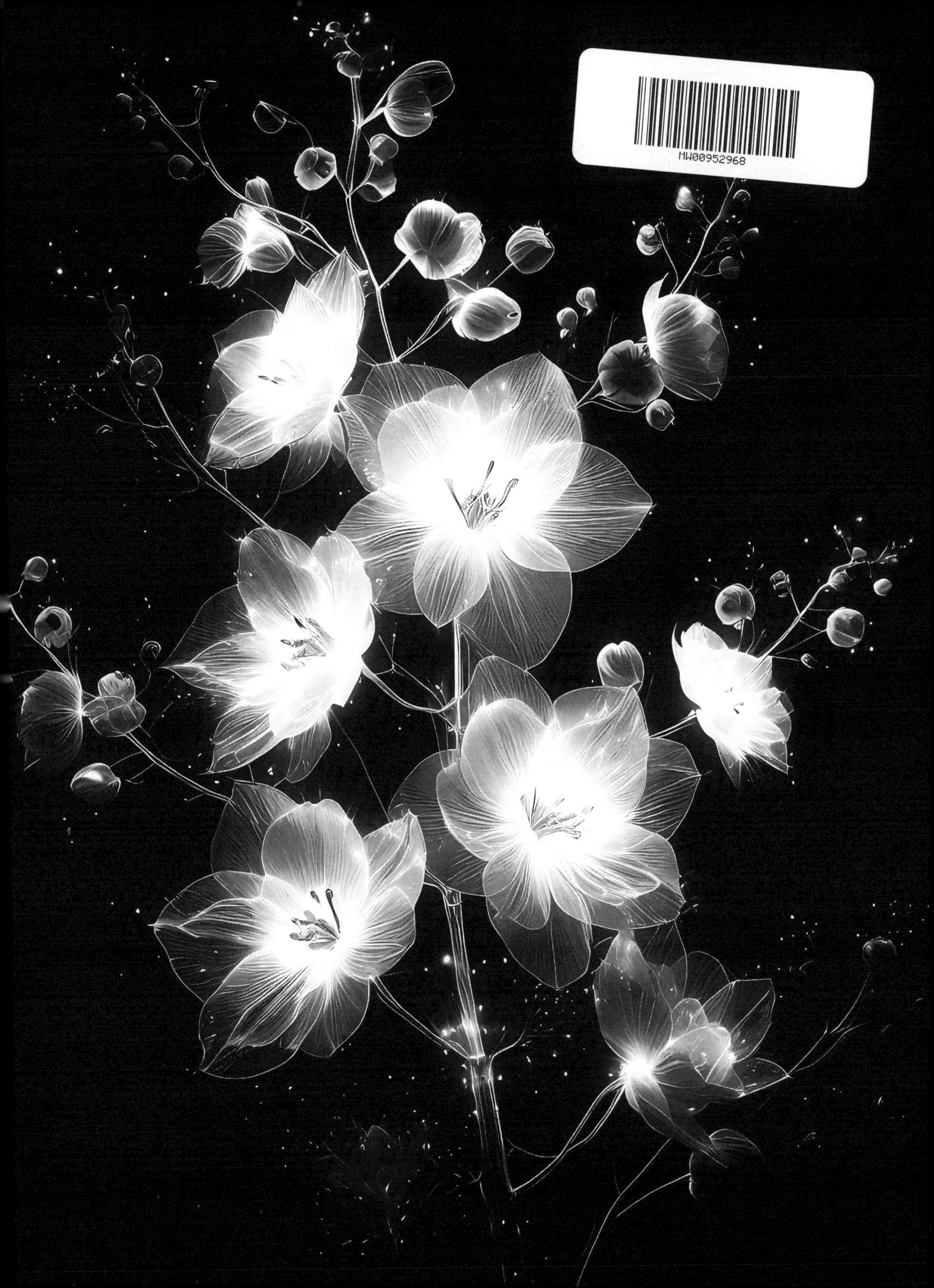

WE'D LOVE TO HEAR YOUR THOUGHTS.

SHARE YOUR HONEST REVIEW HERE:

Your support means the world to us.

Mast vibe books

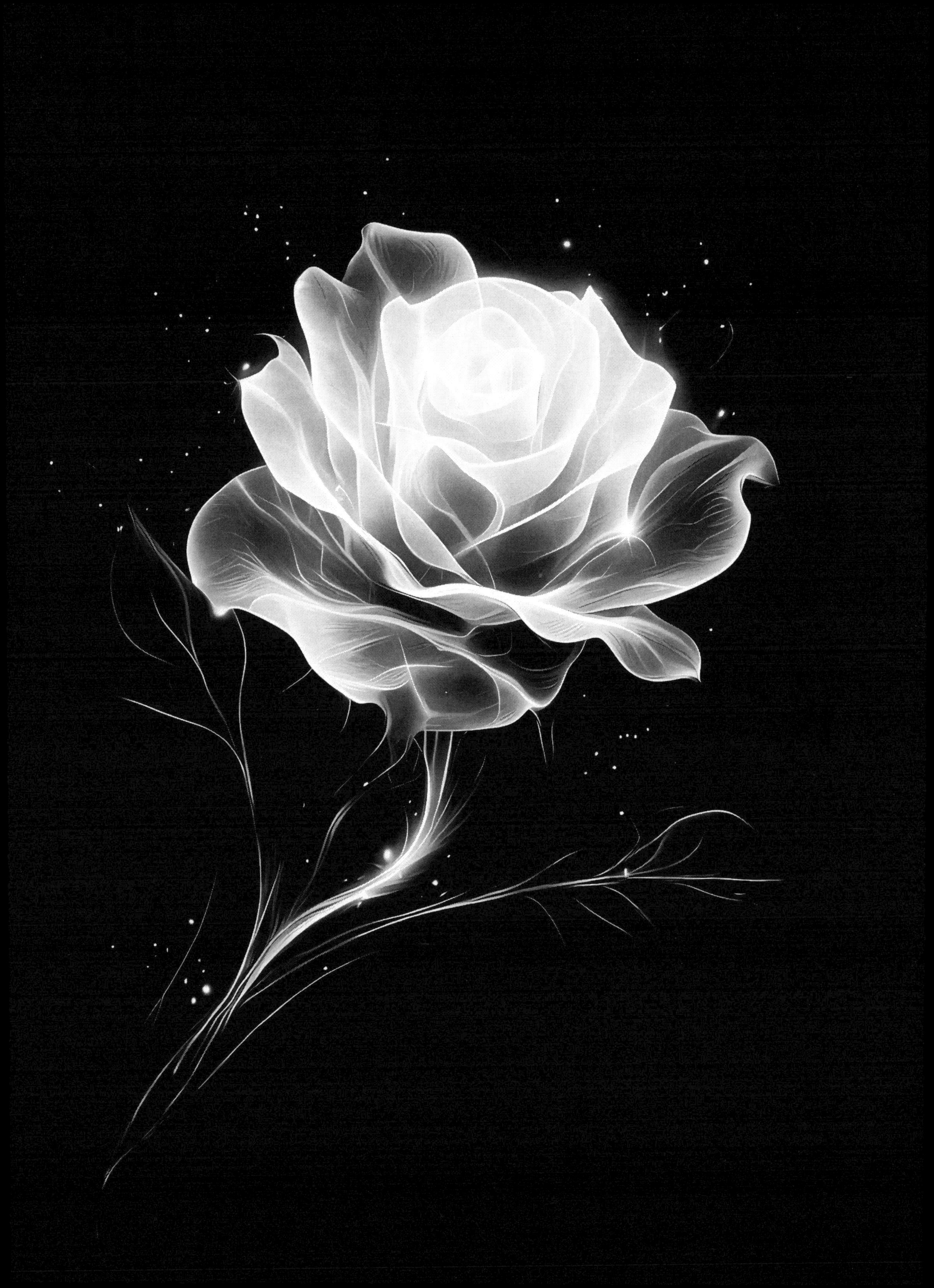

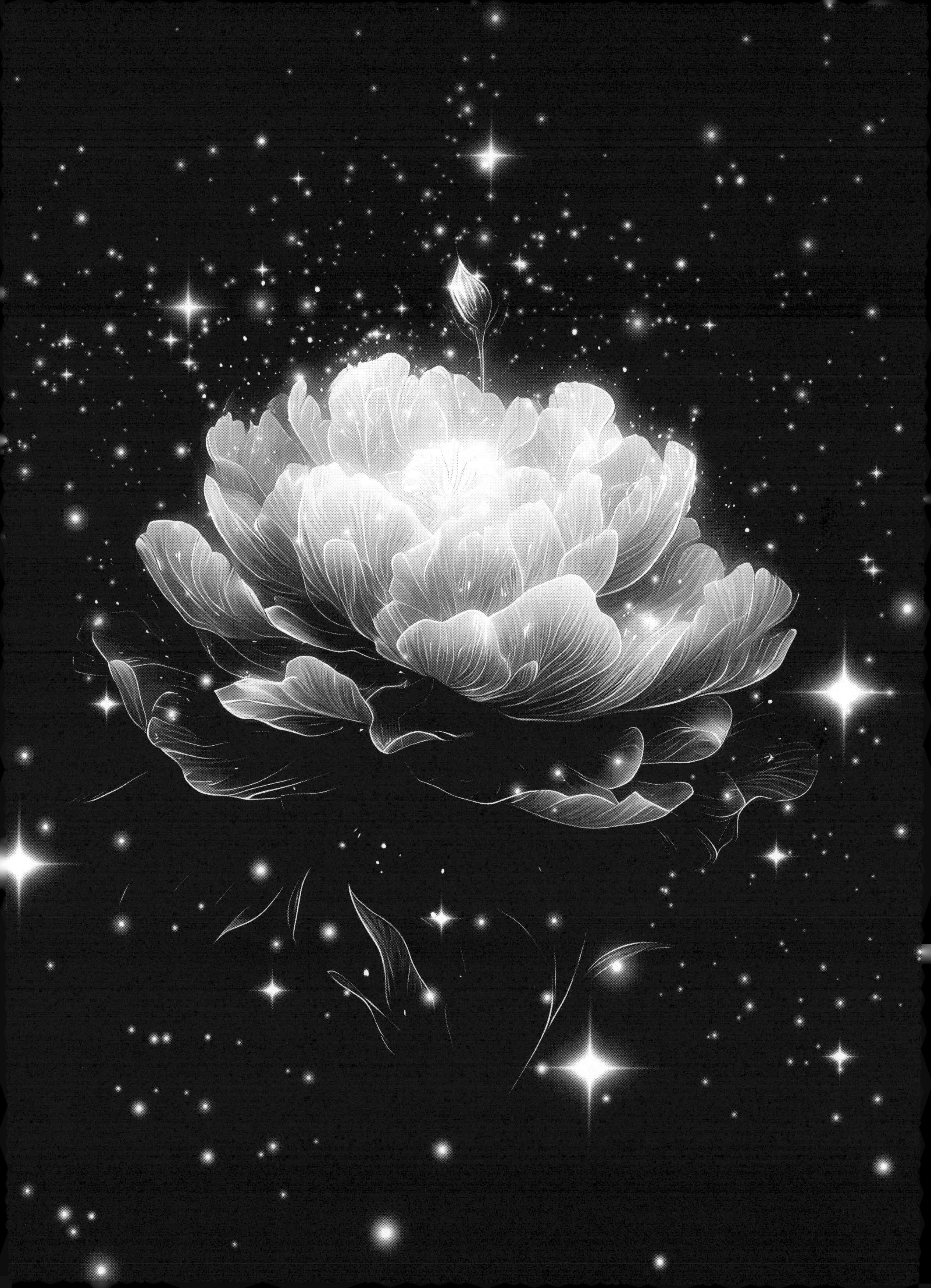

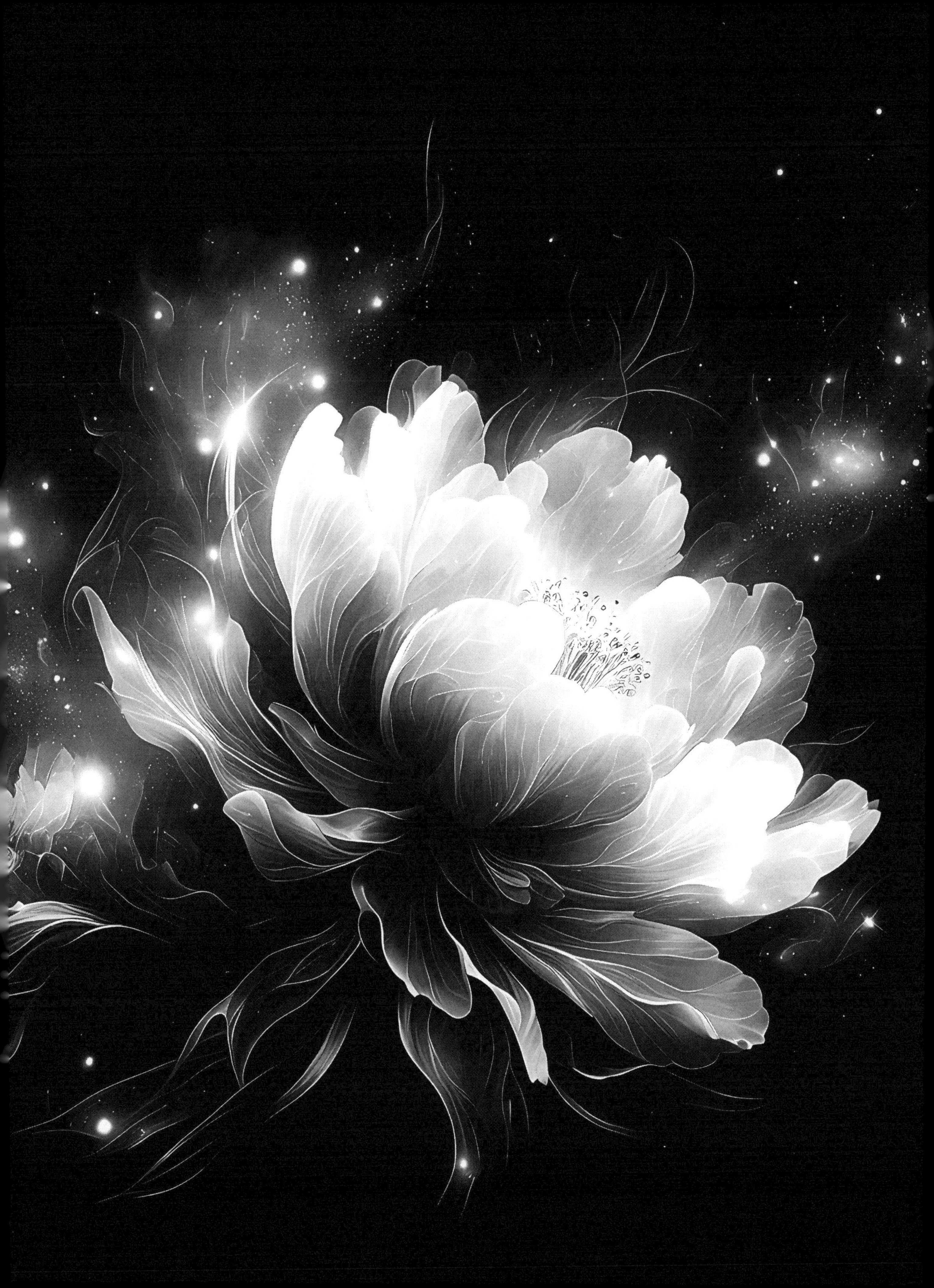

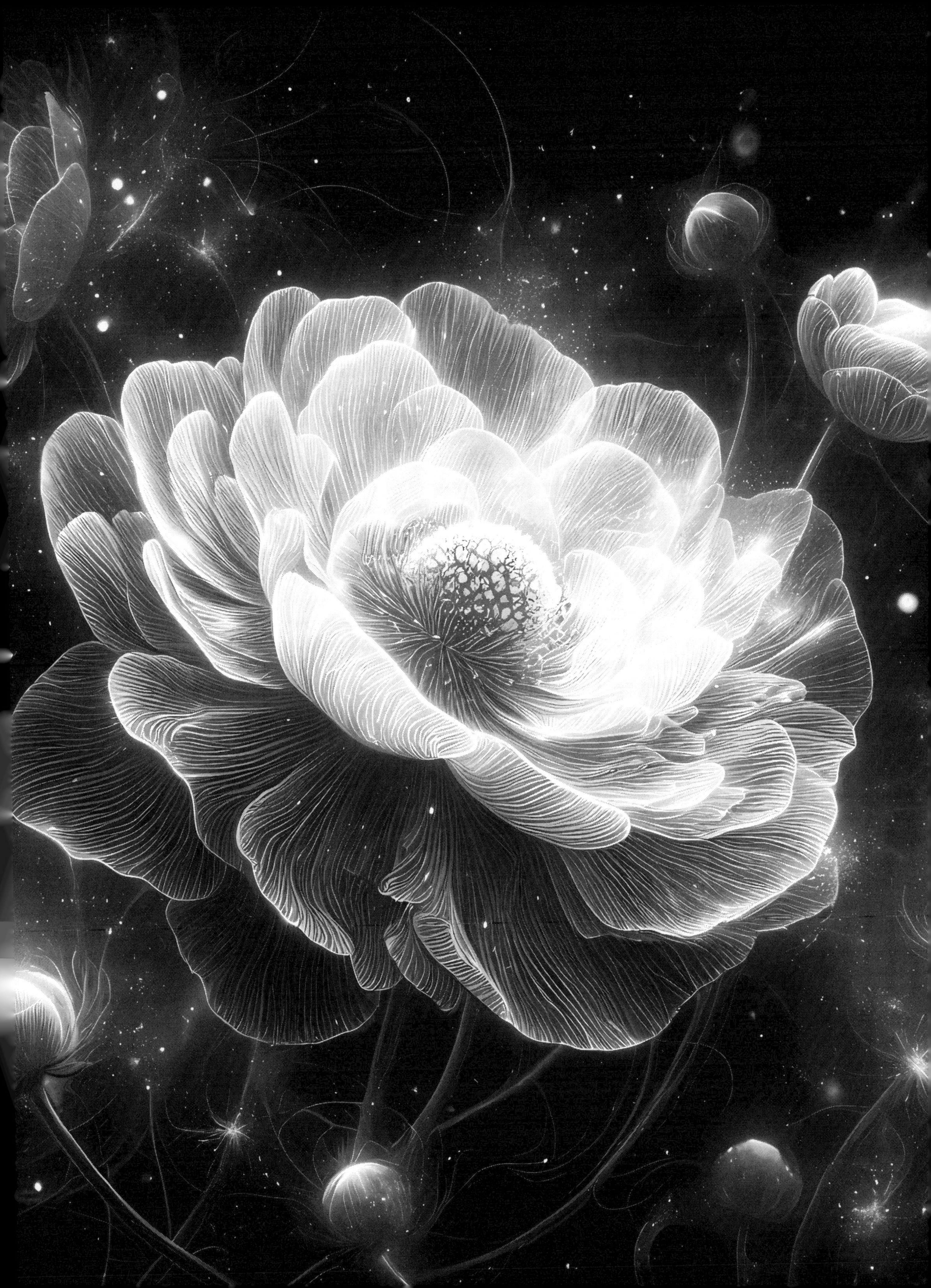

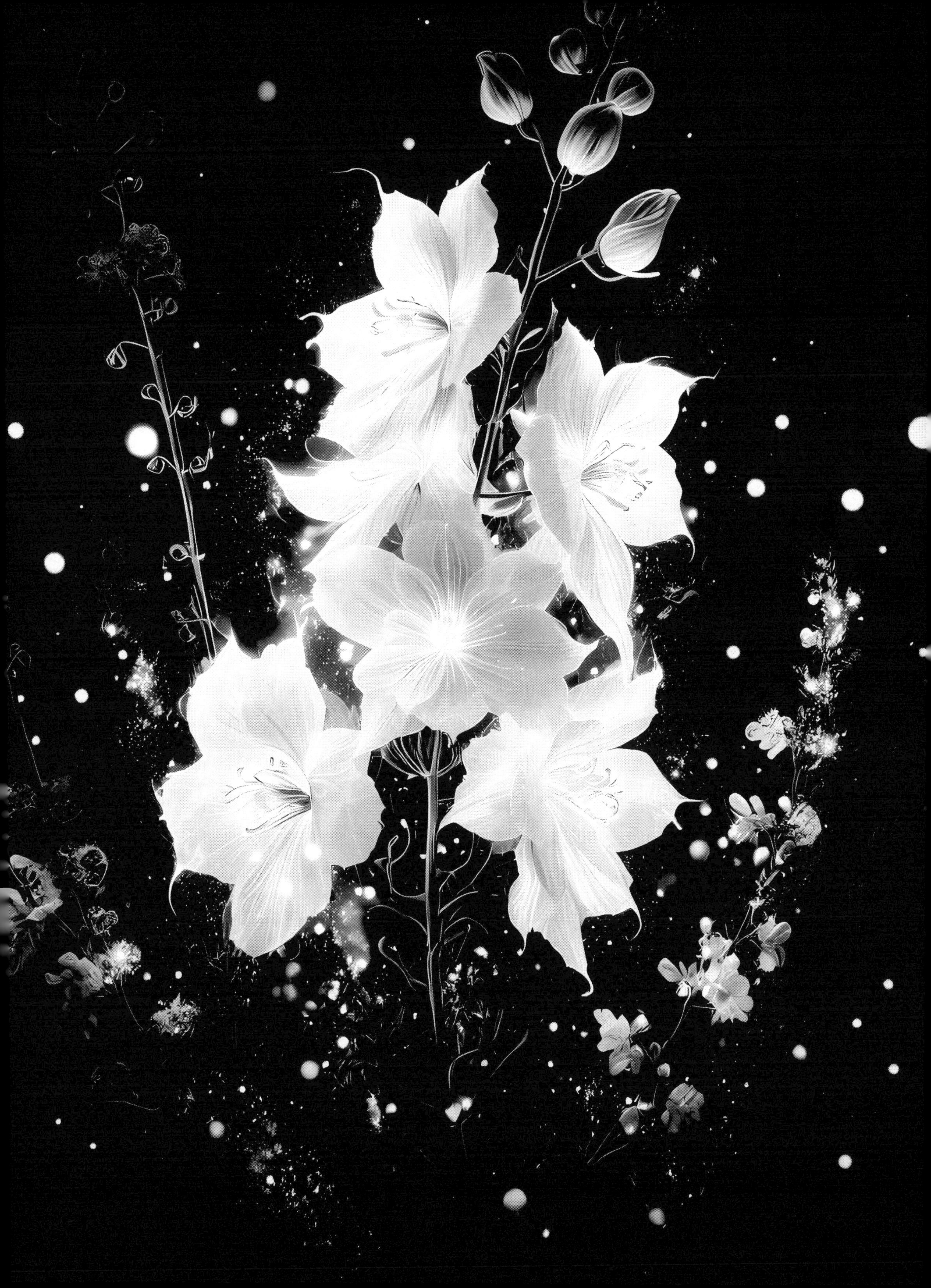

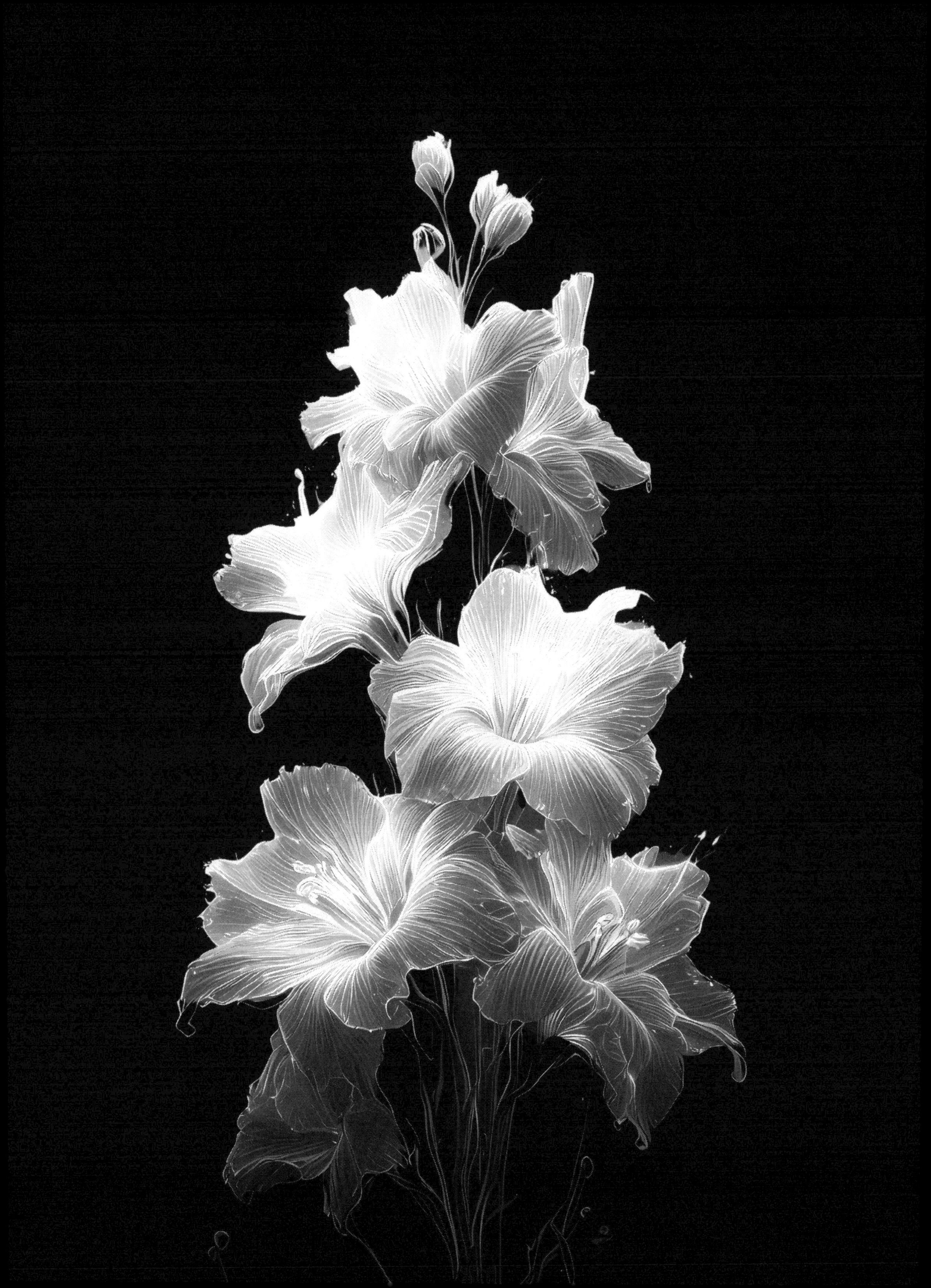

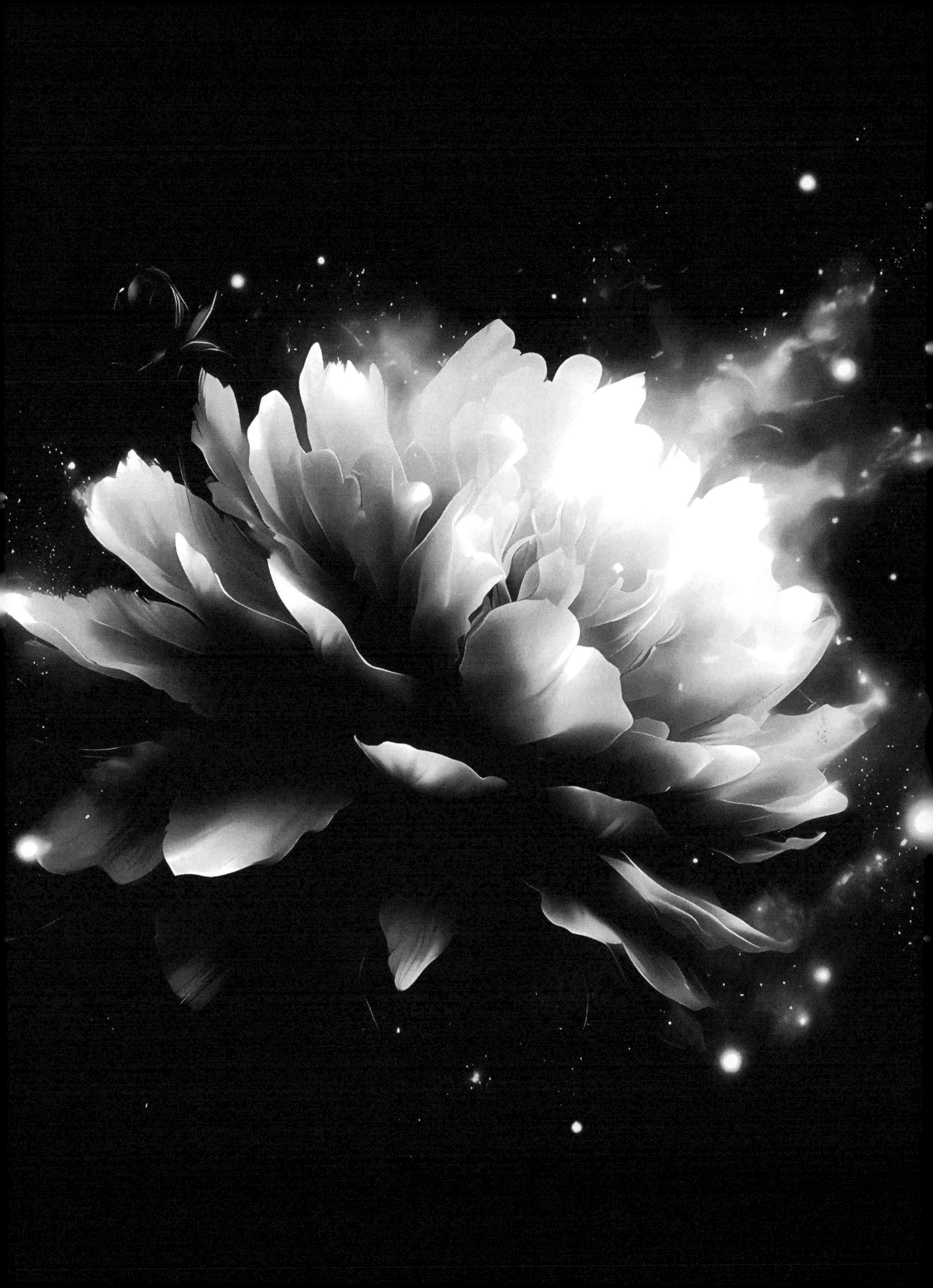

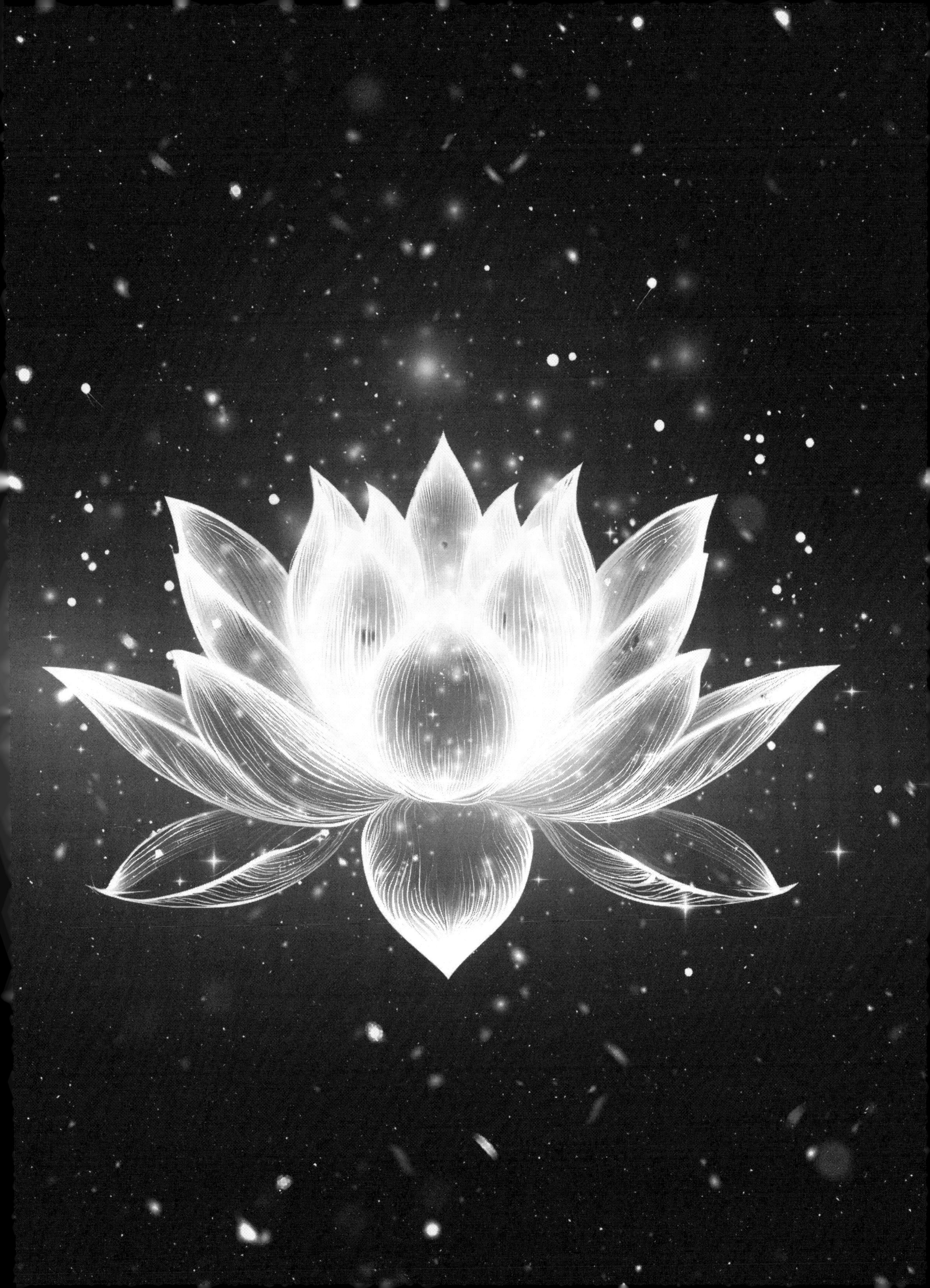

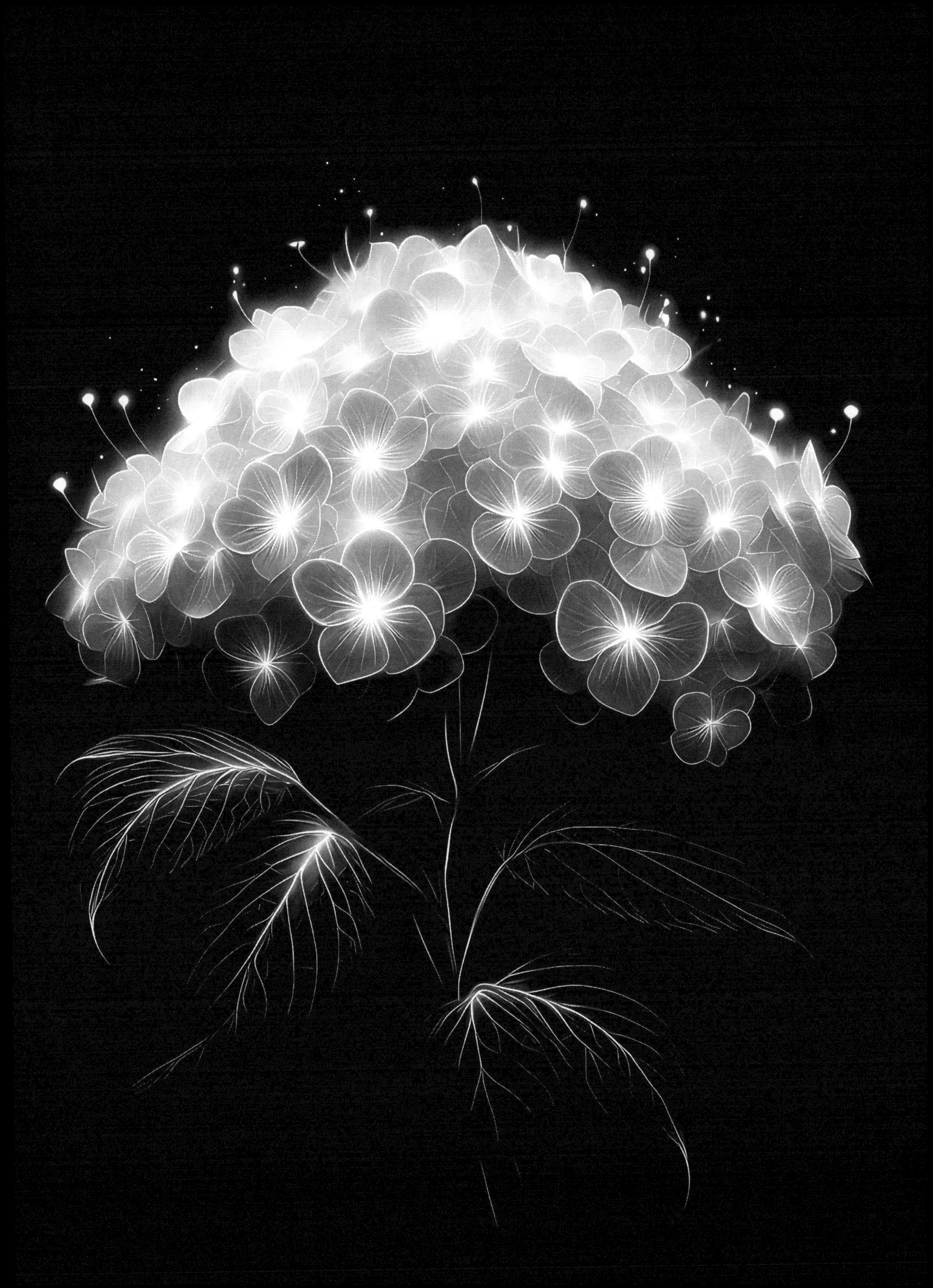

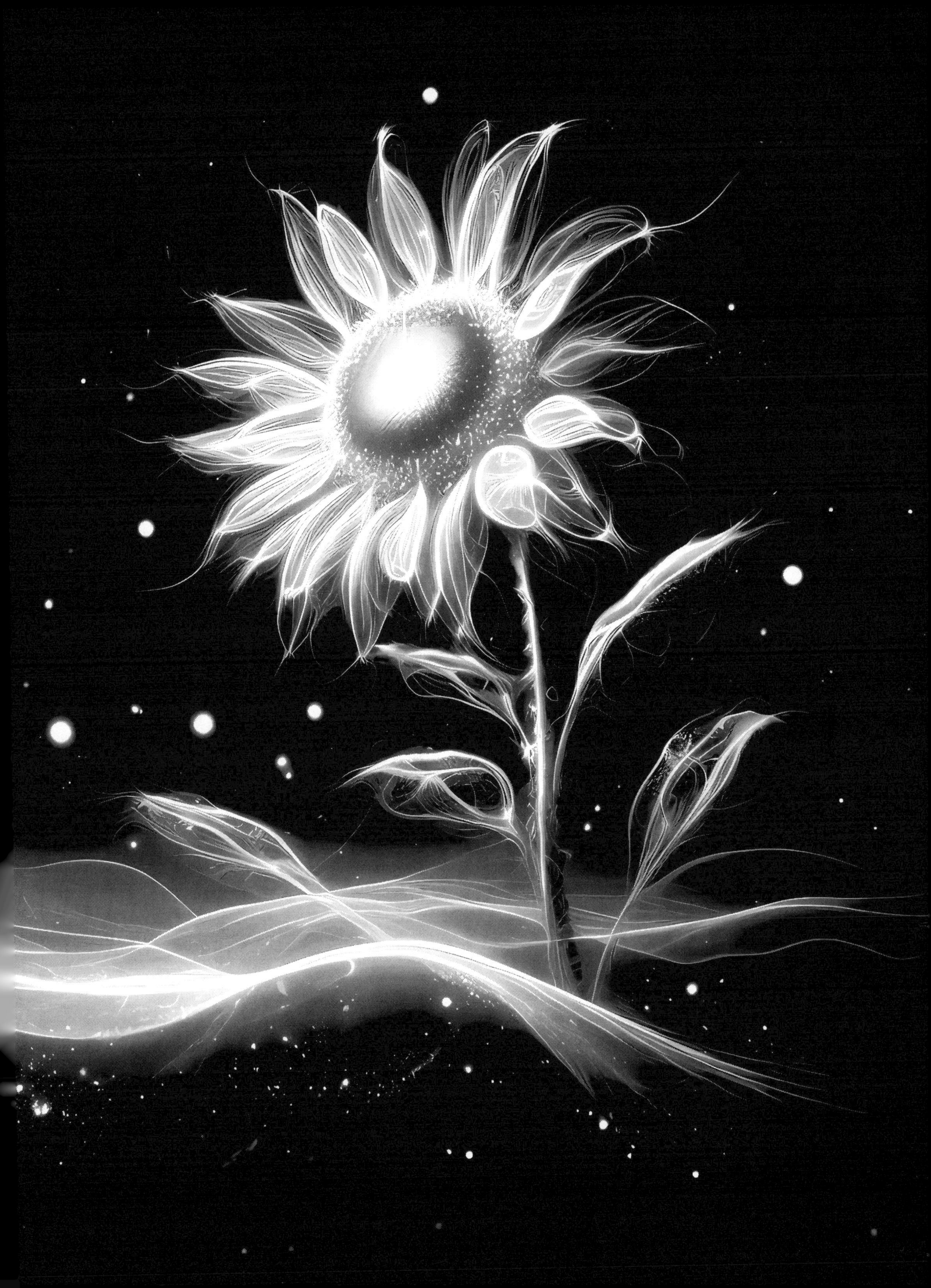

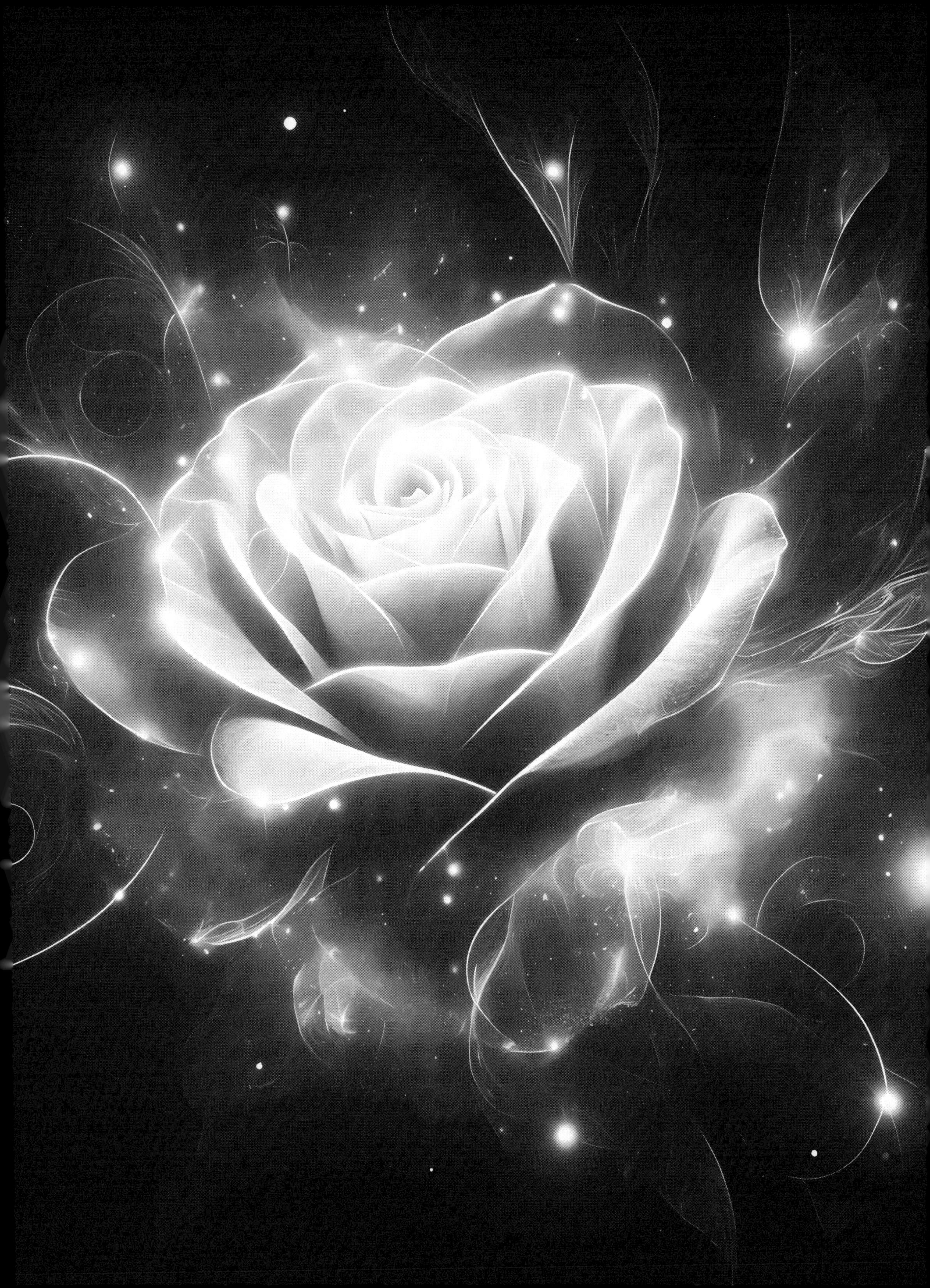

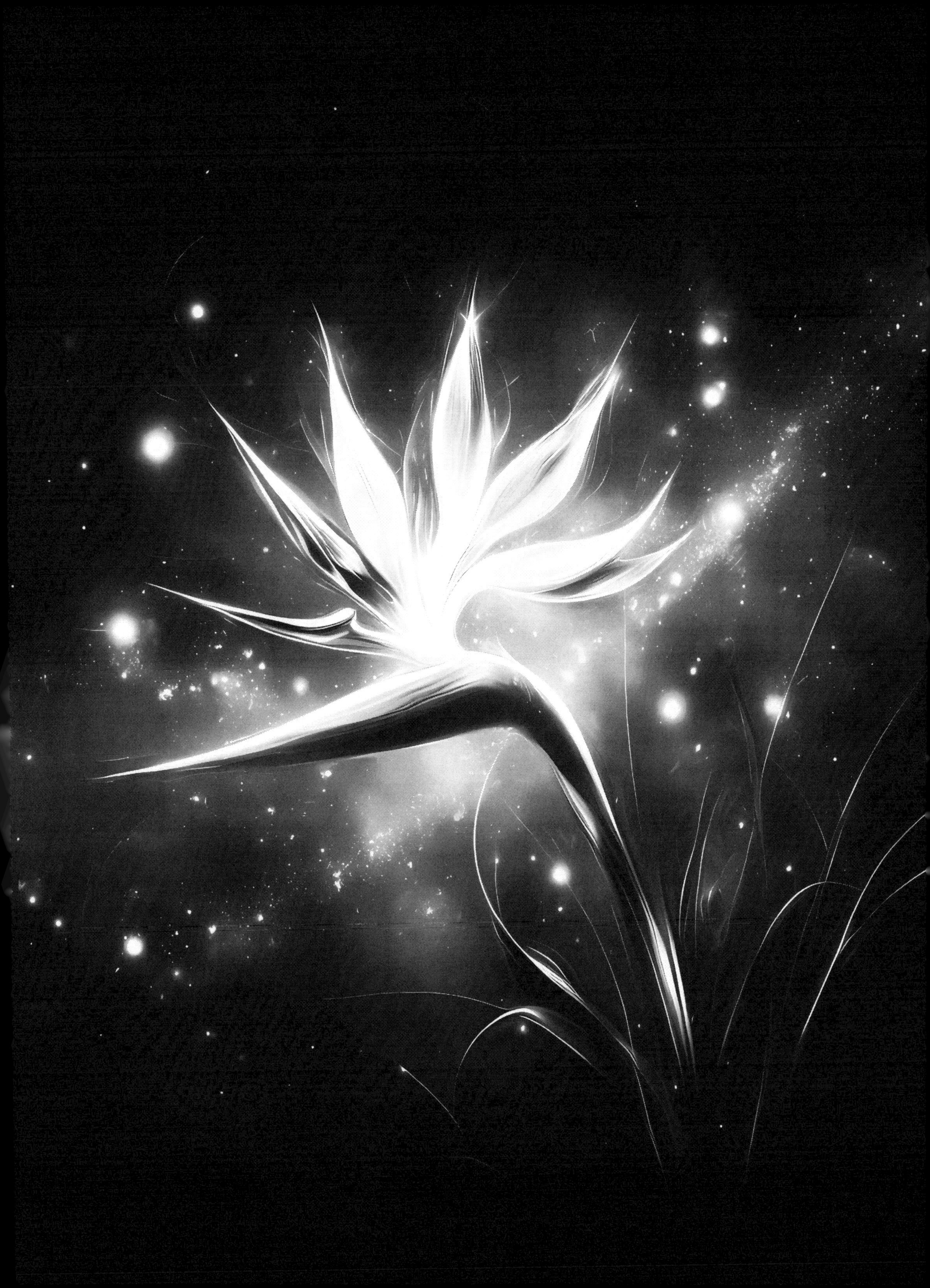

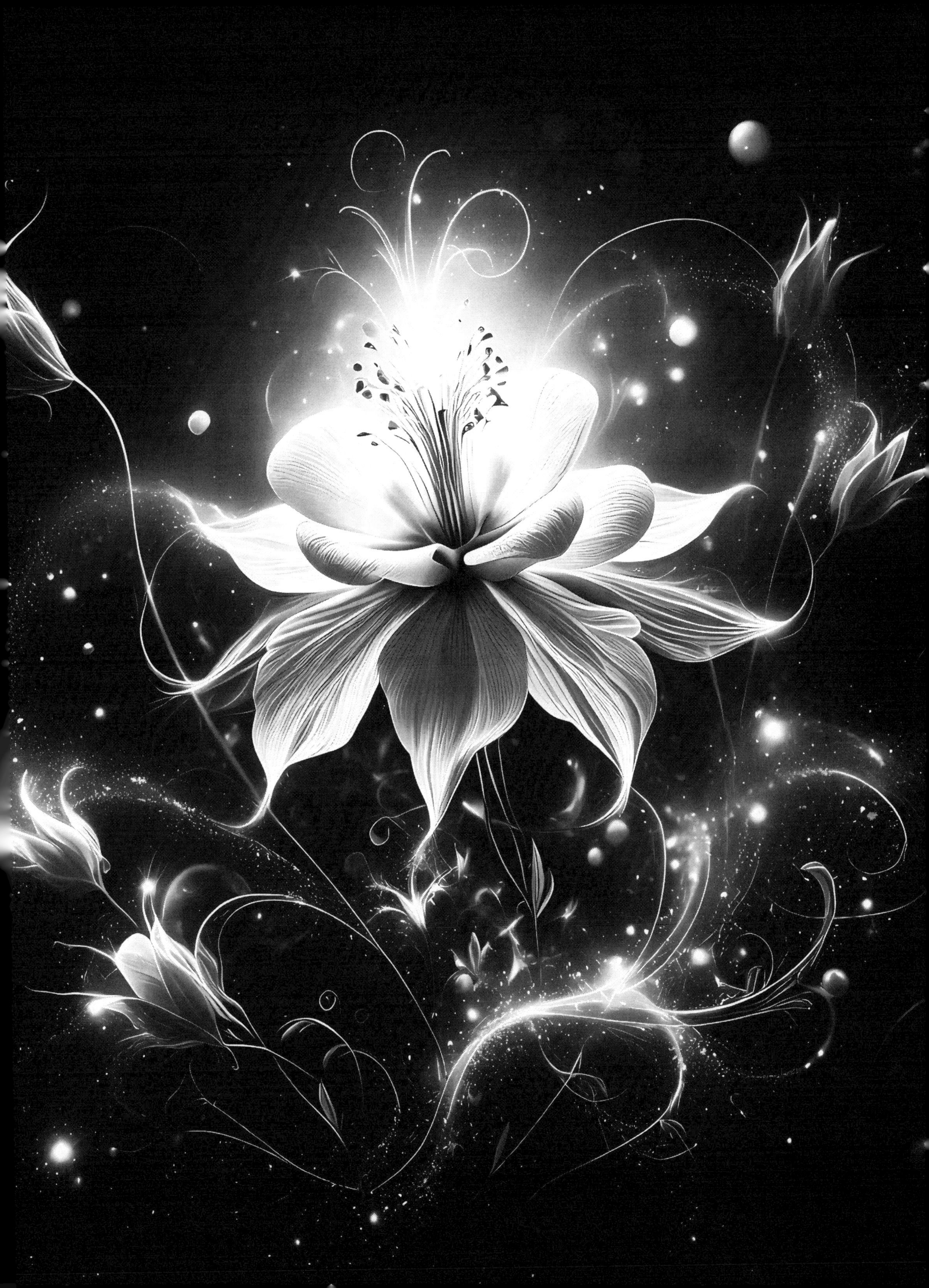

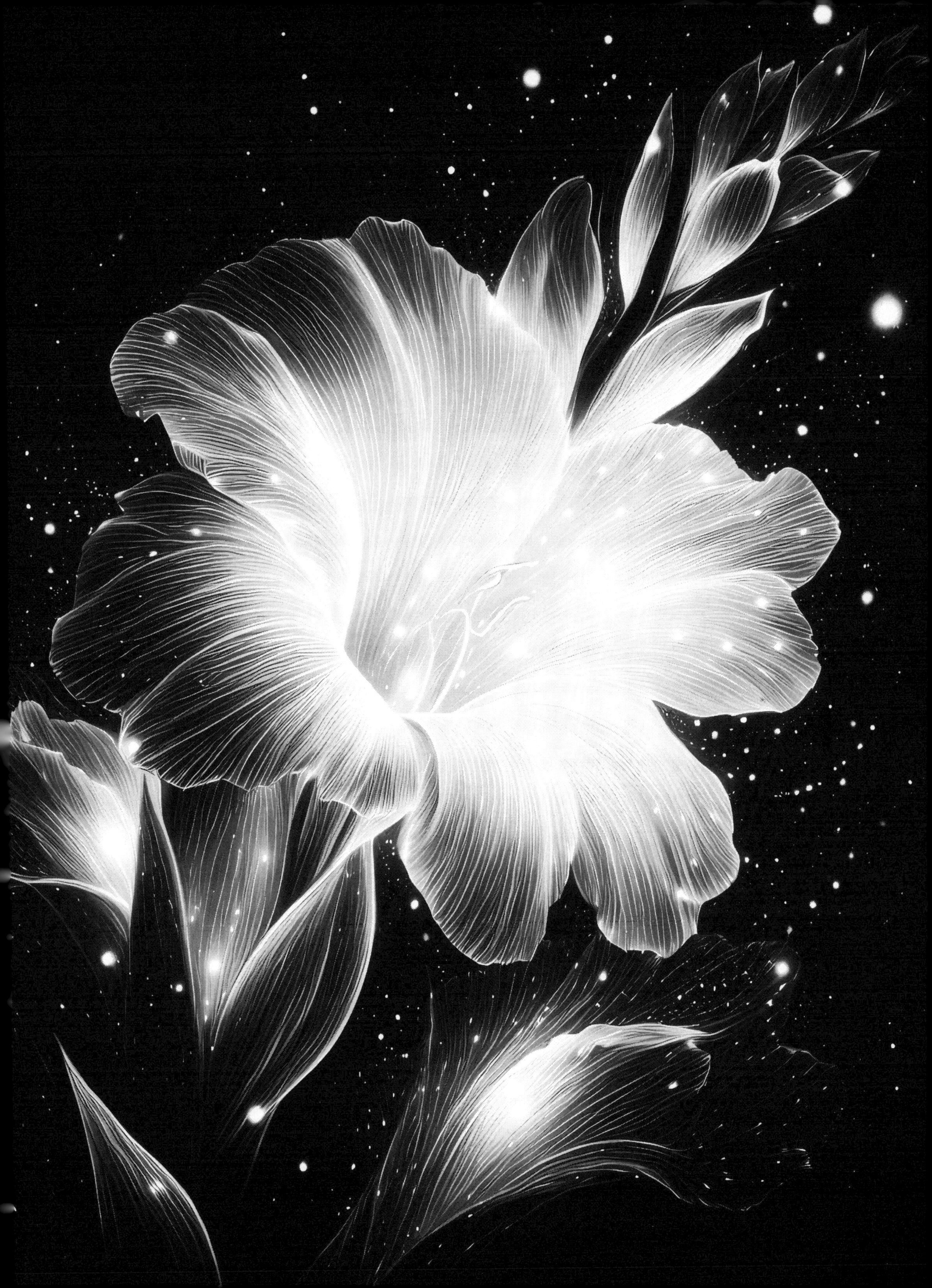

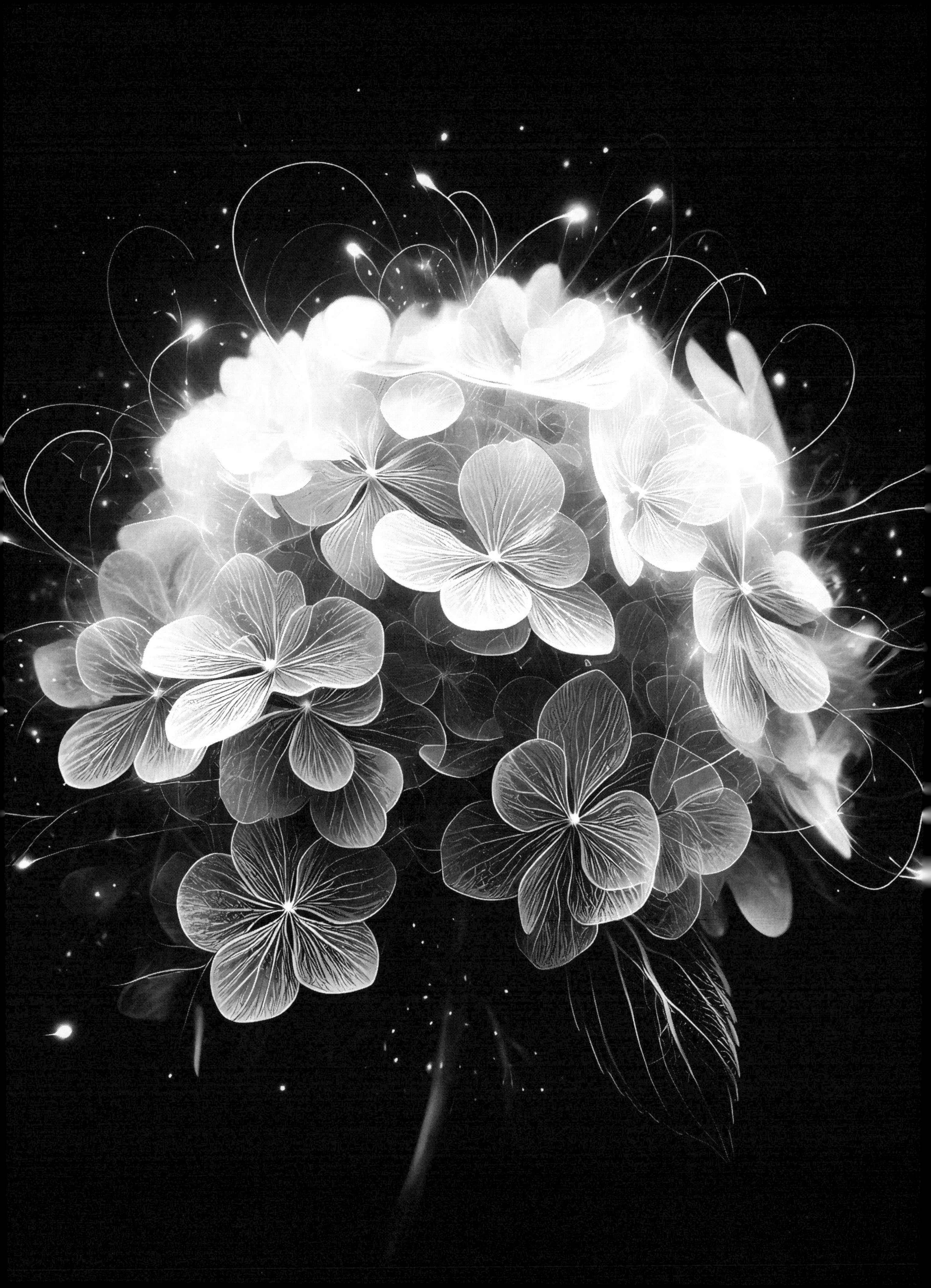

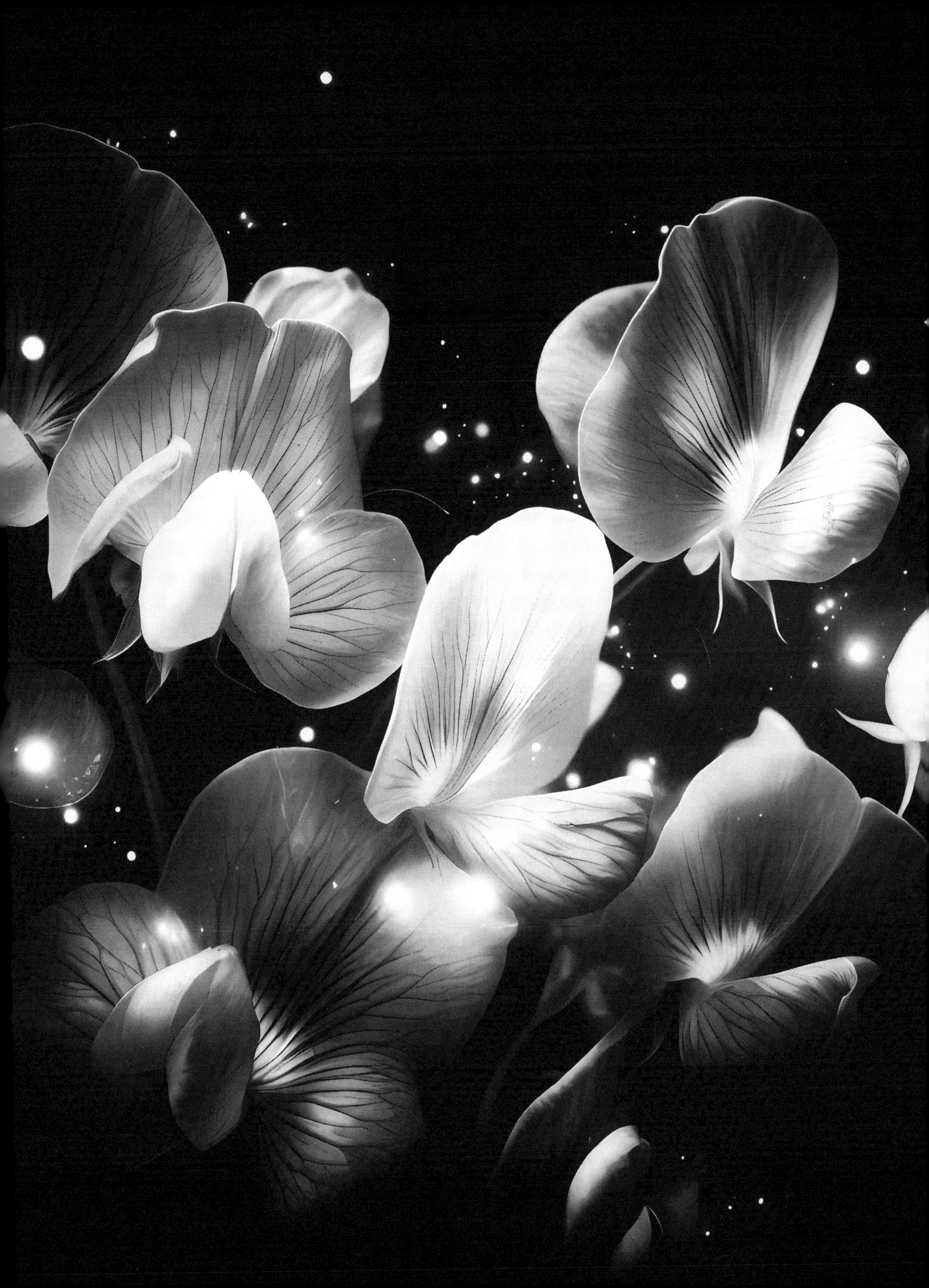

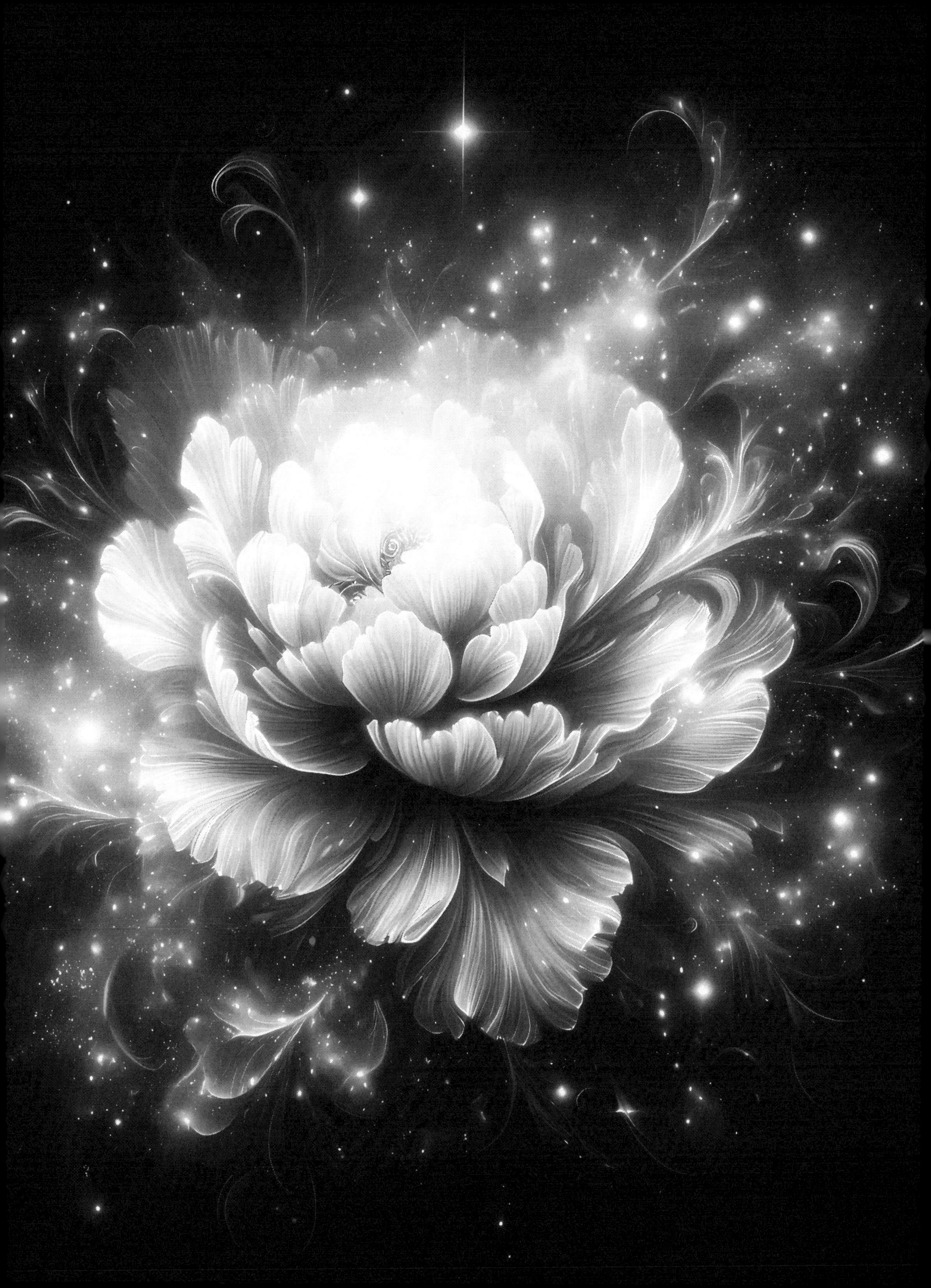

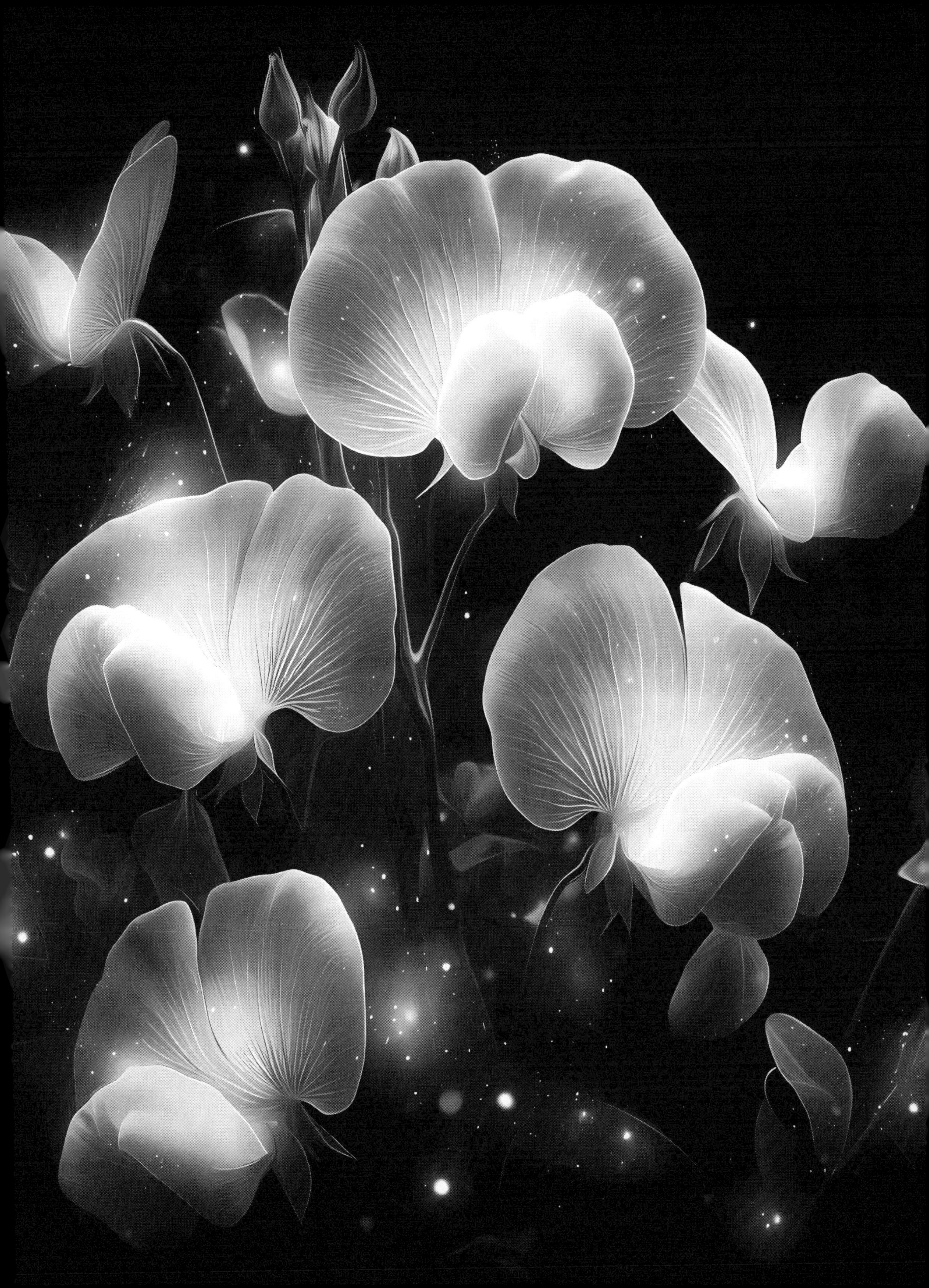

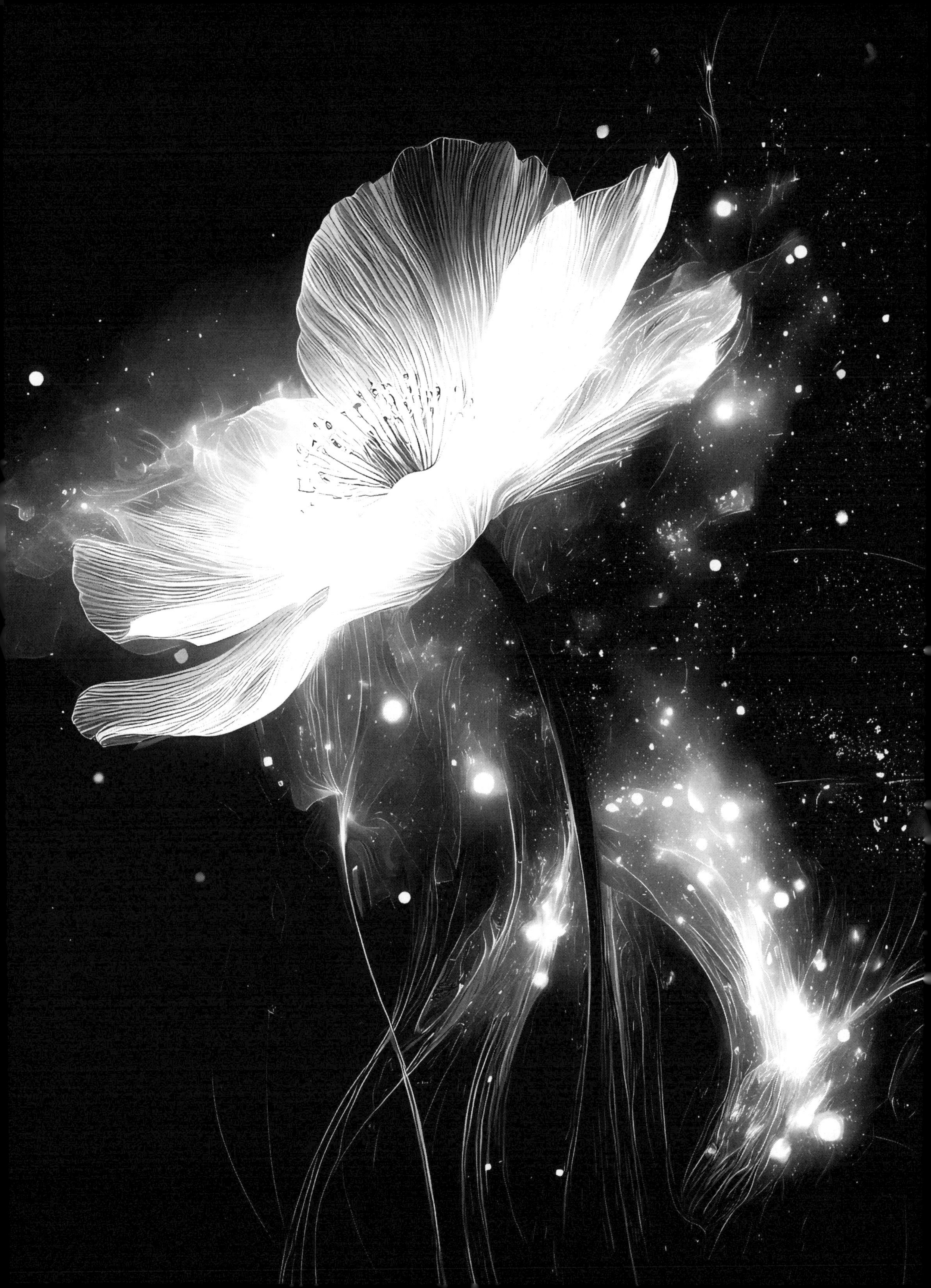

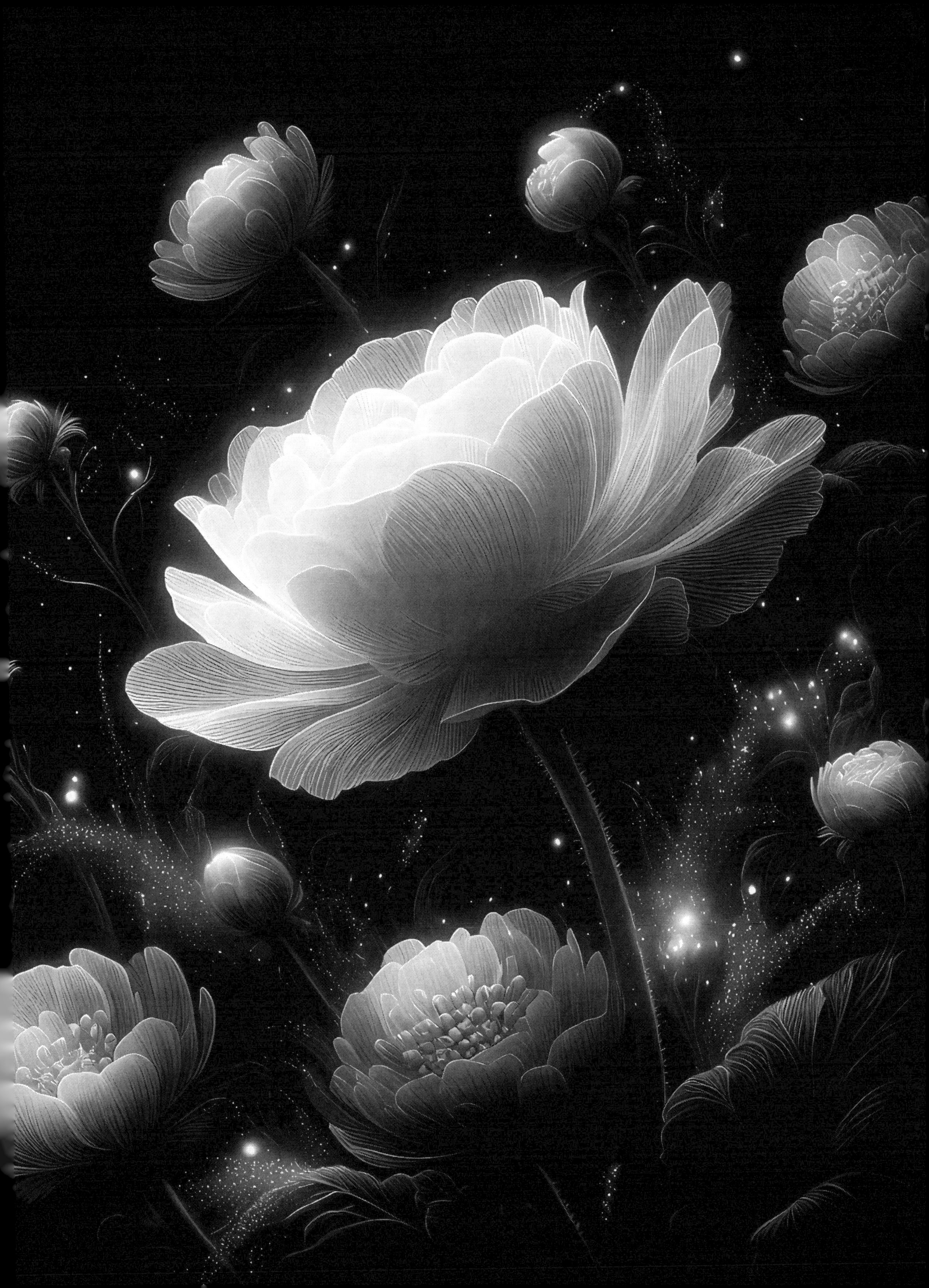

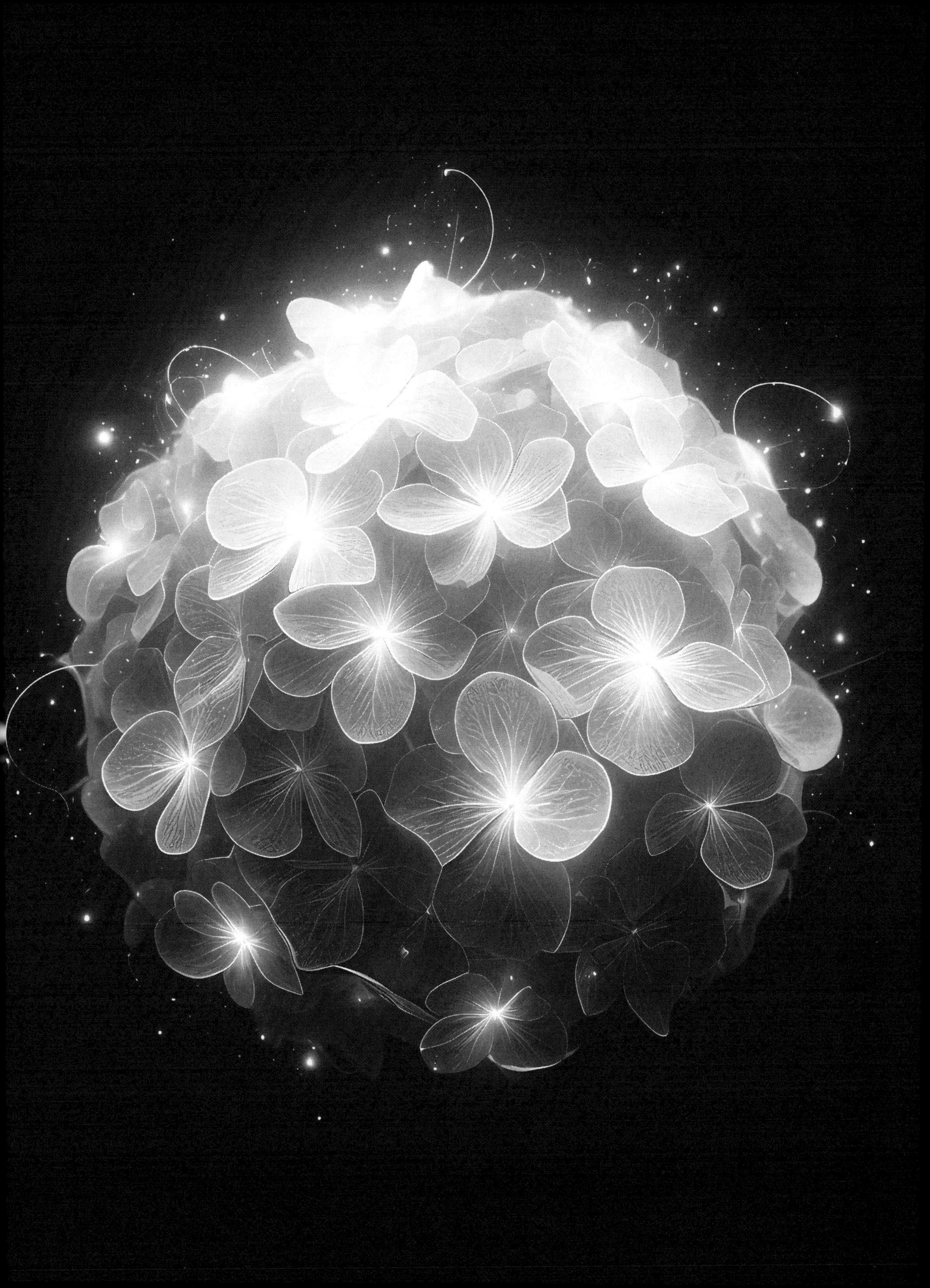

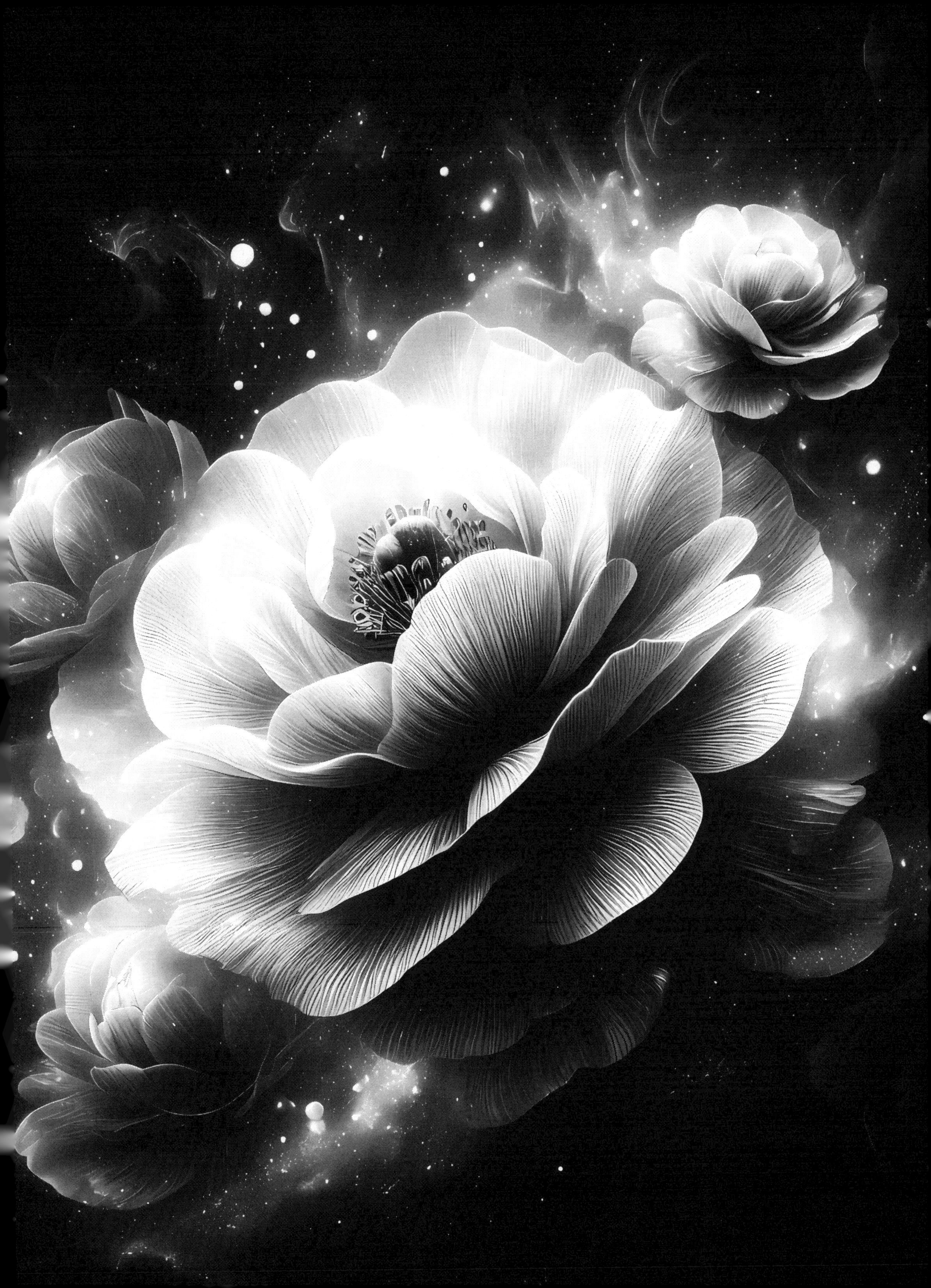

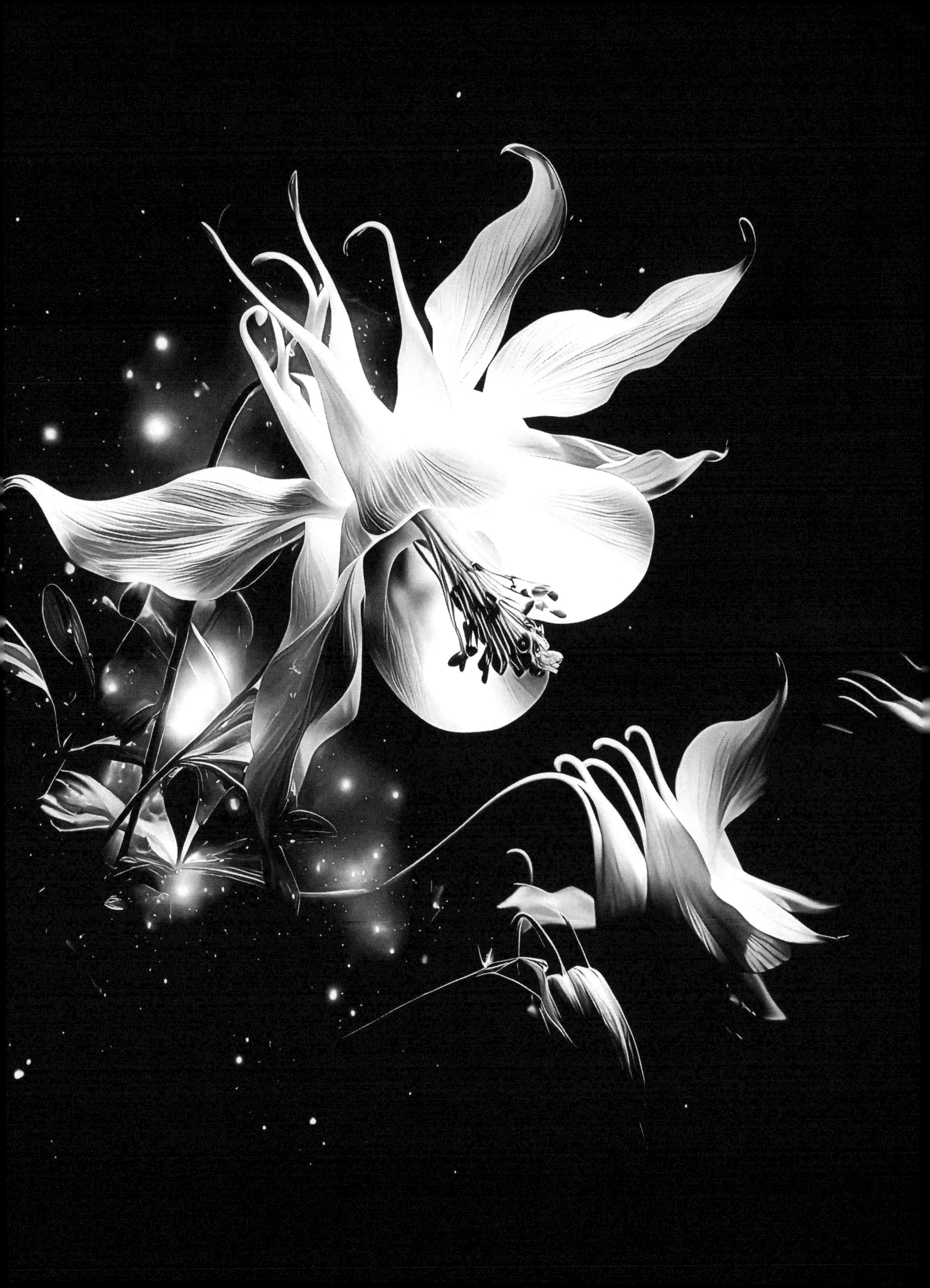

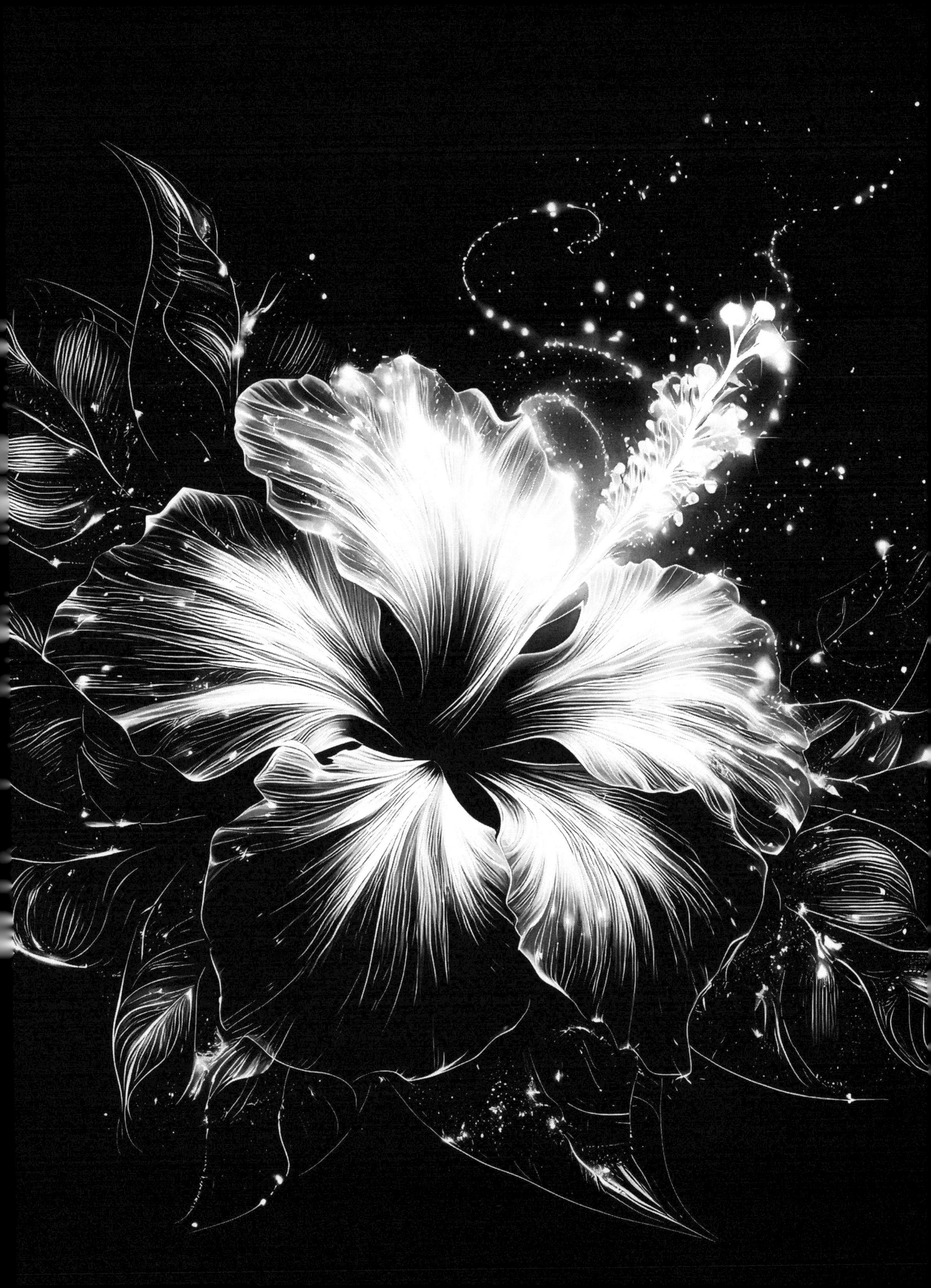

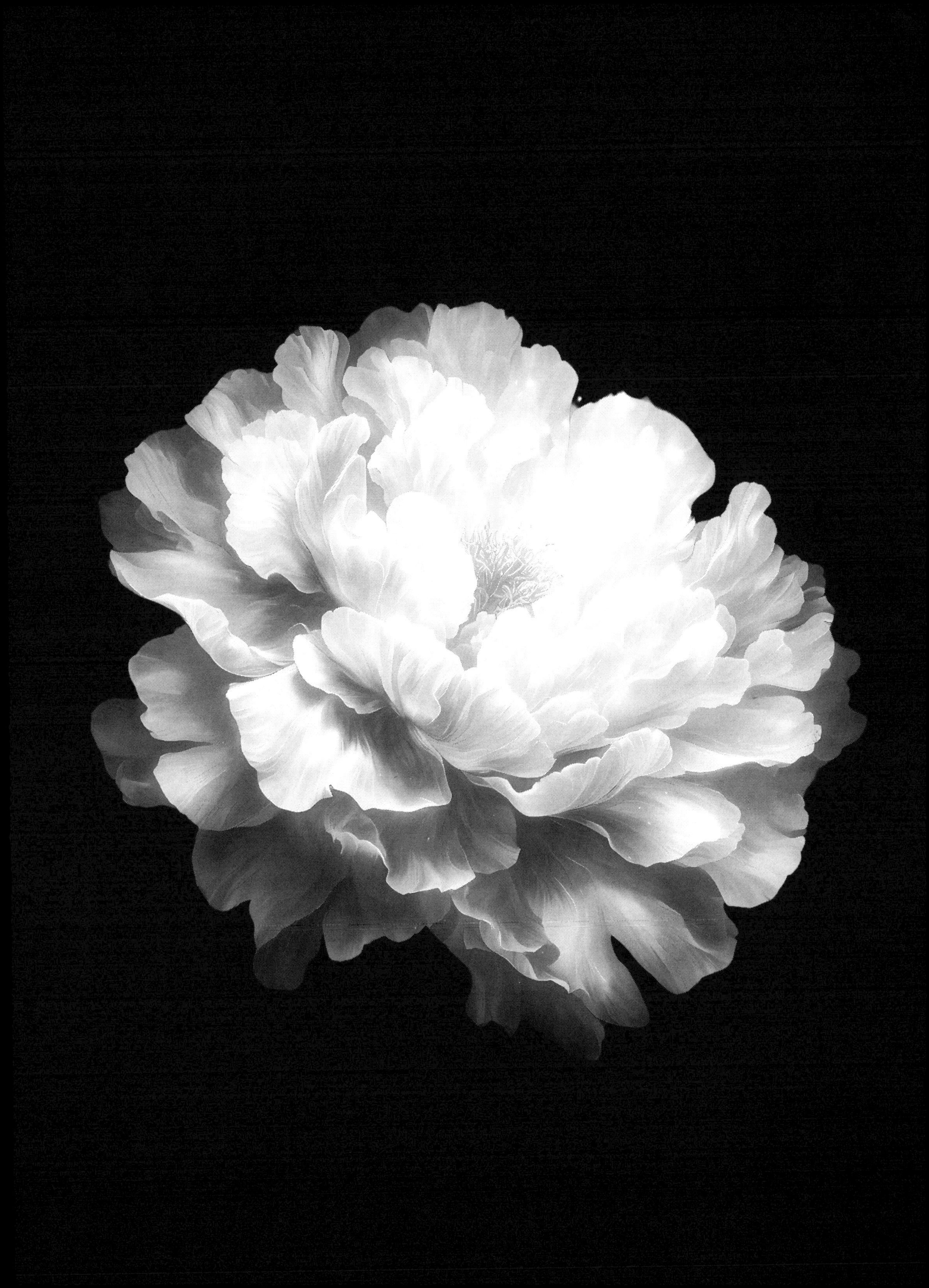

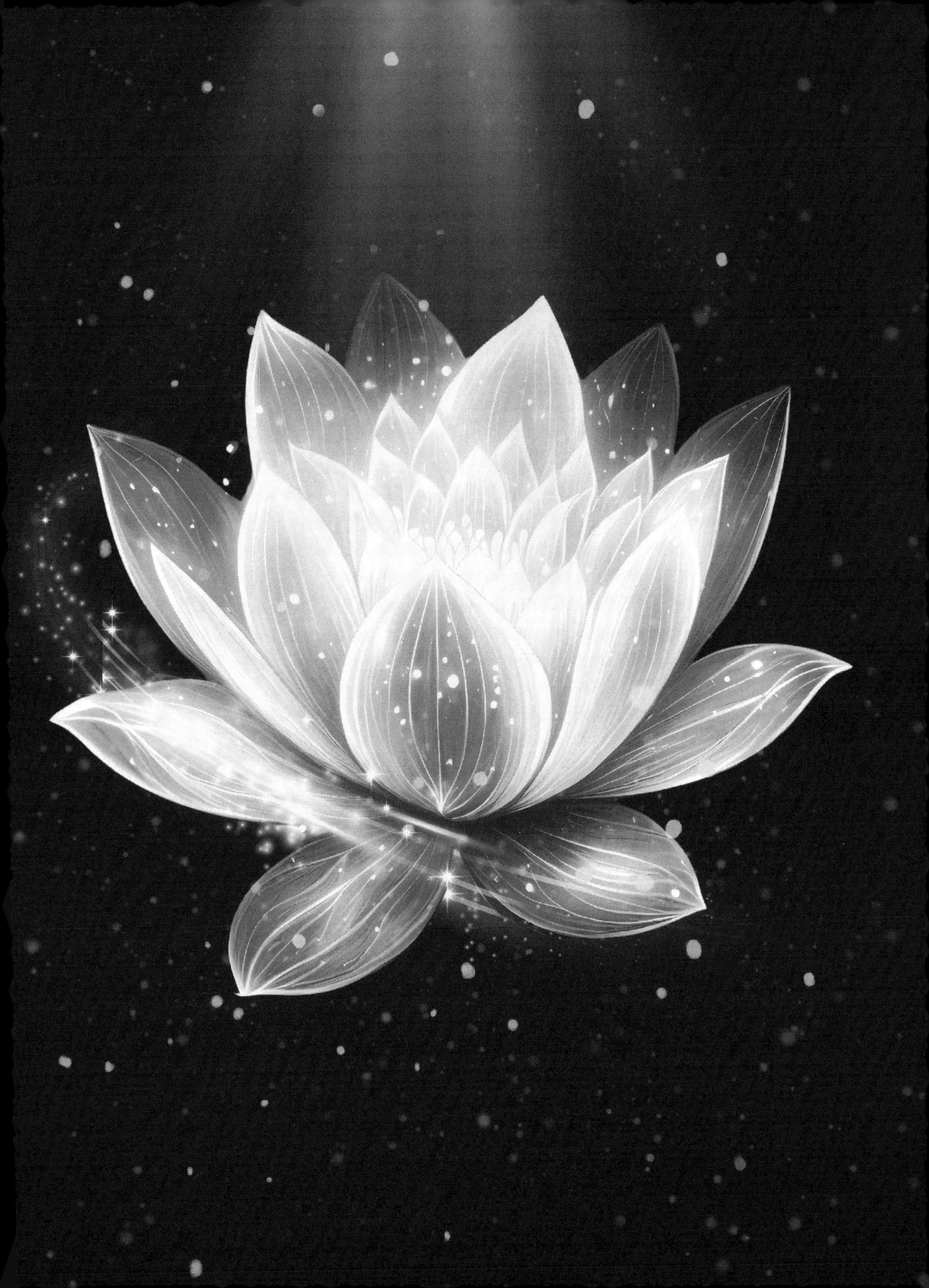

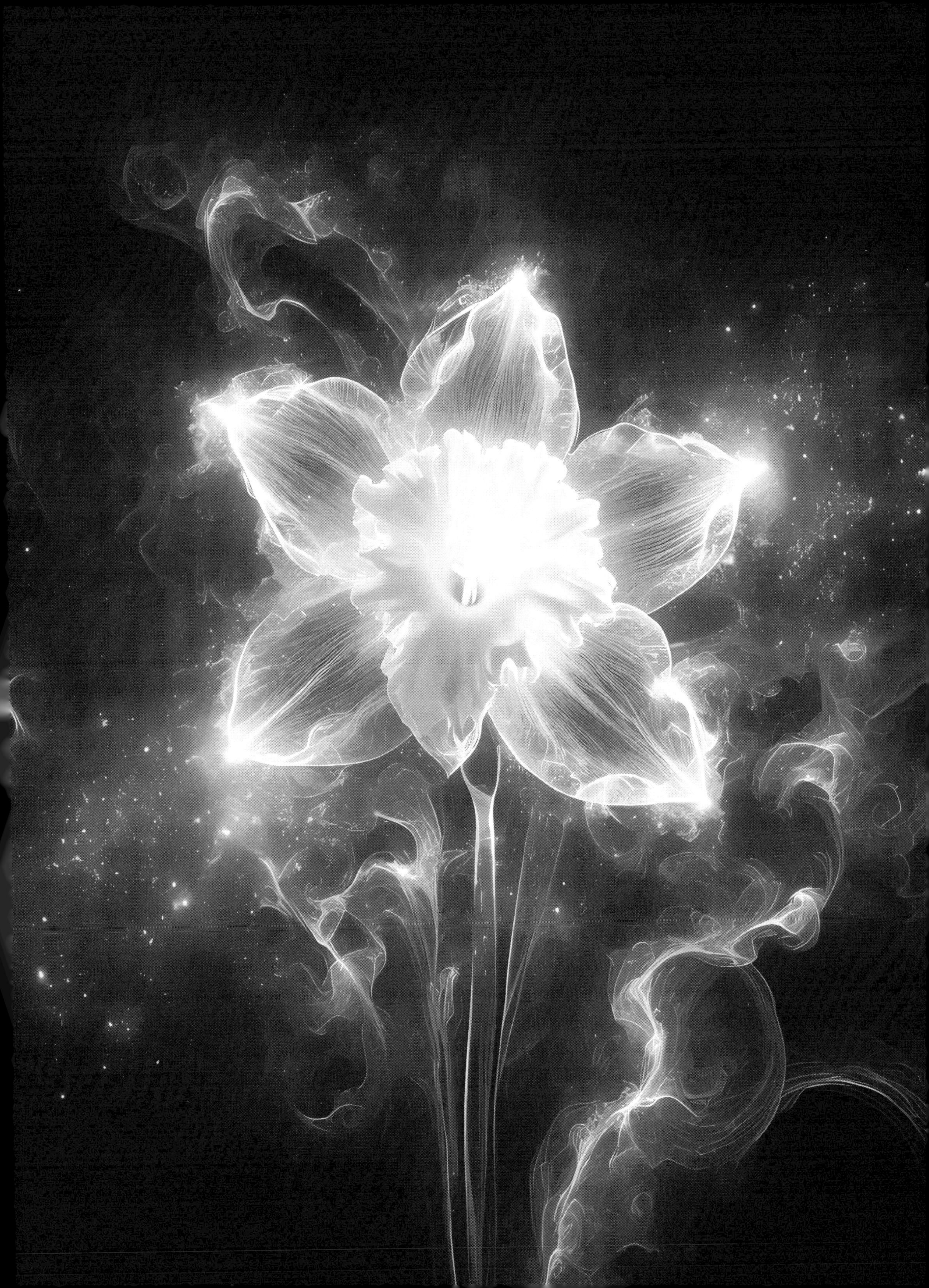

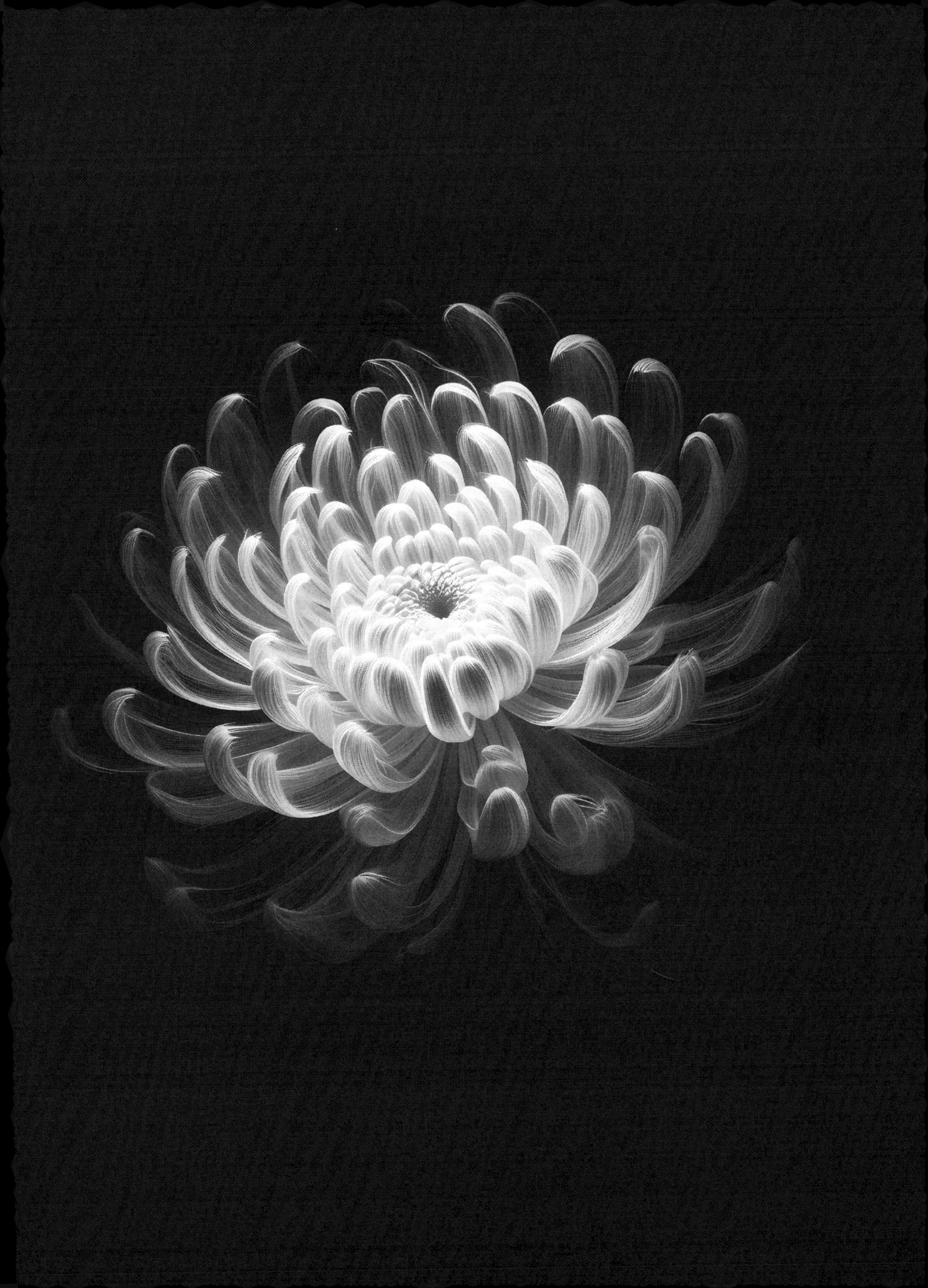

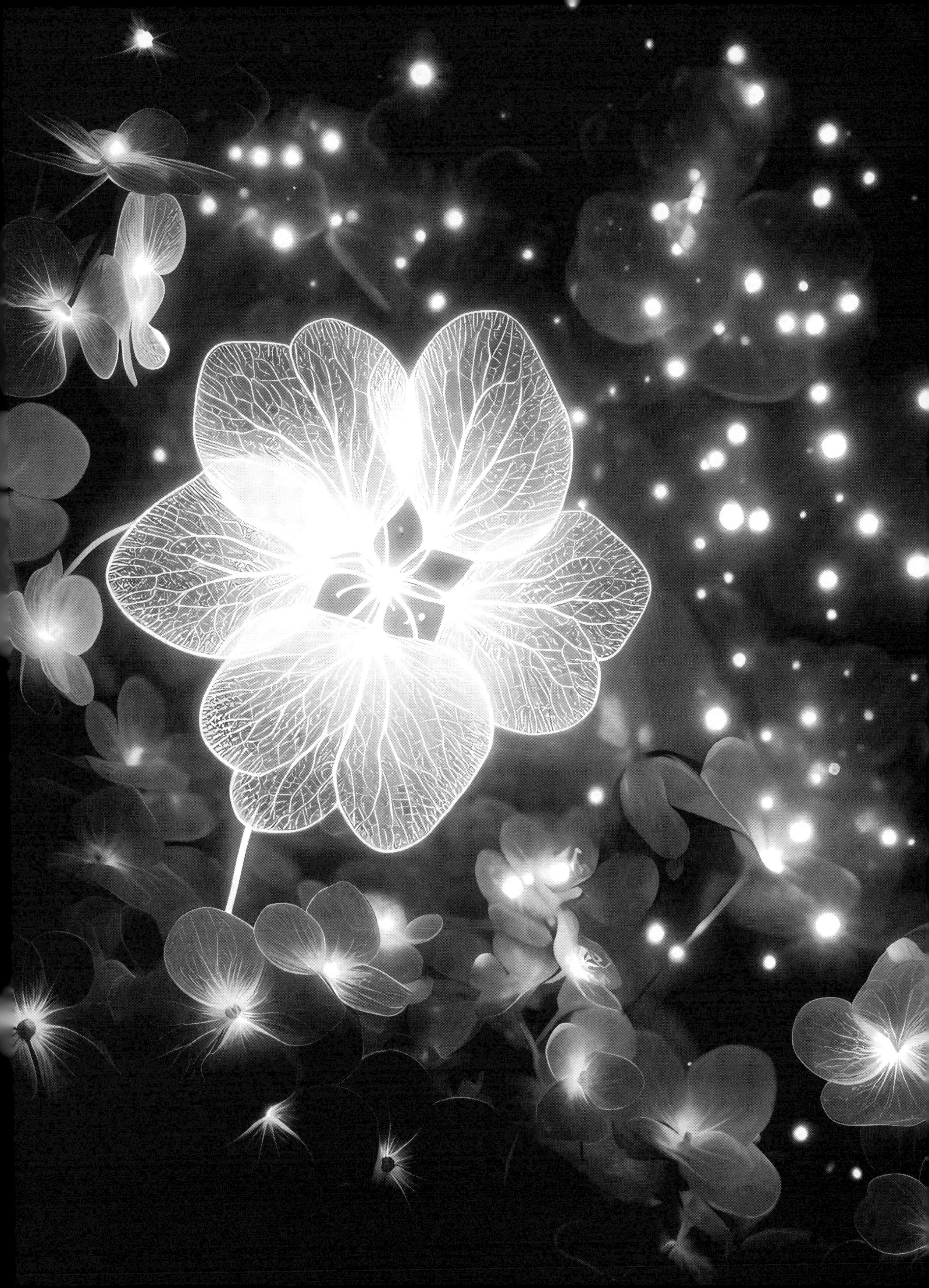

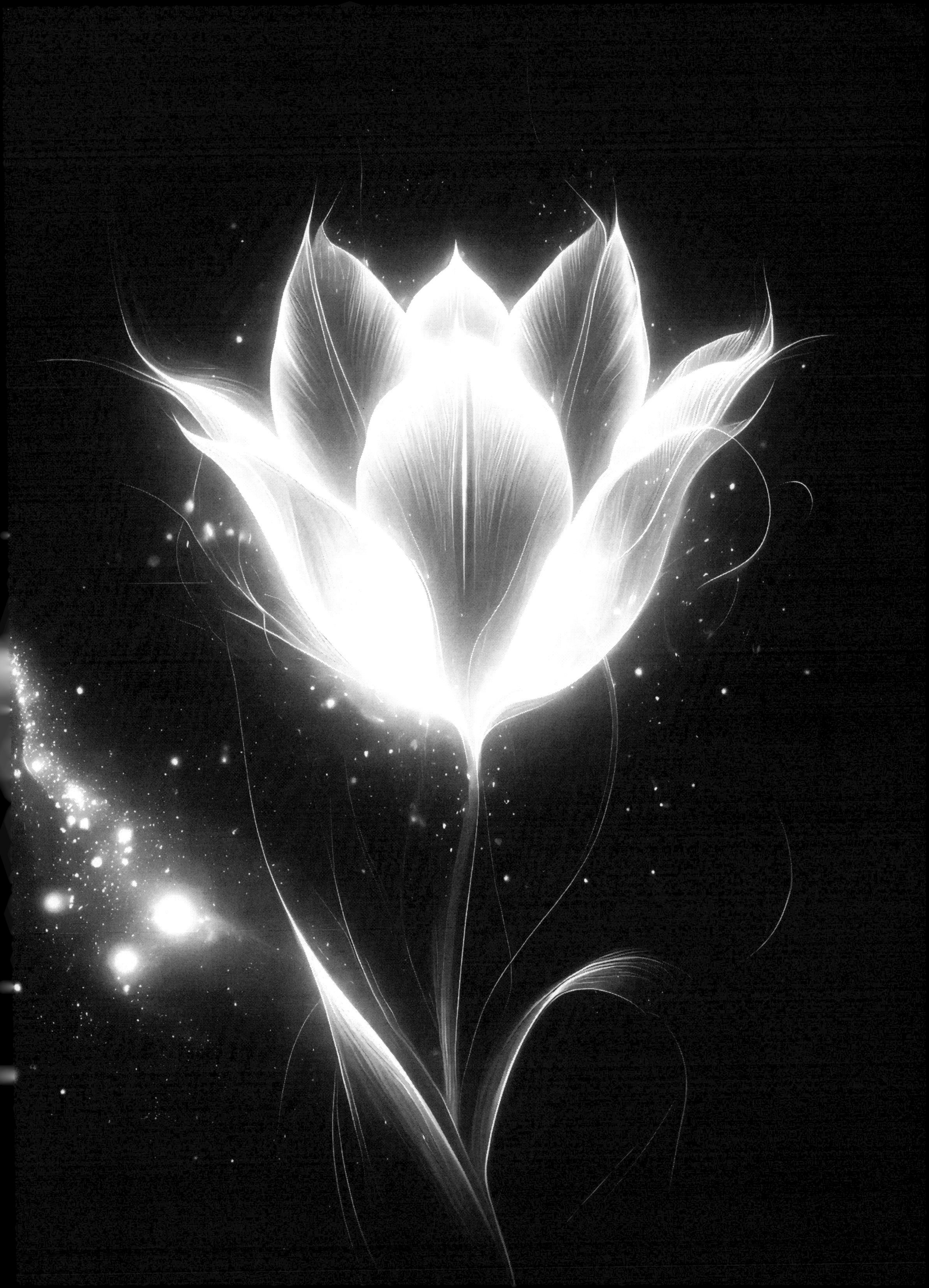

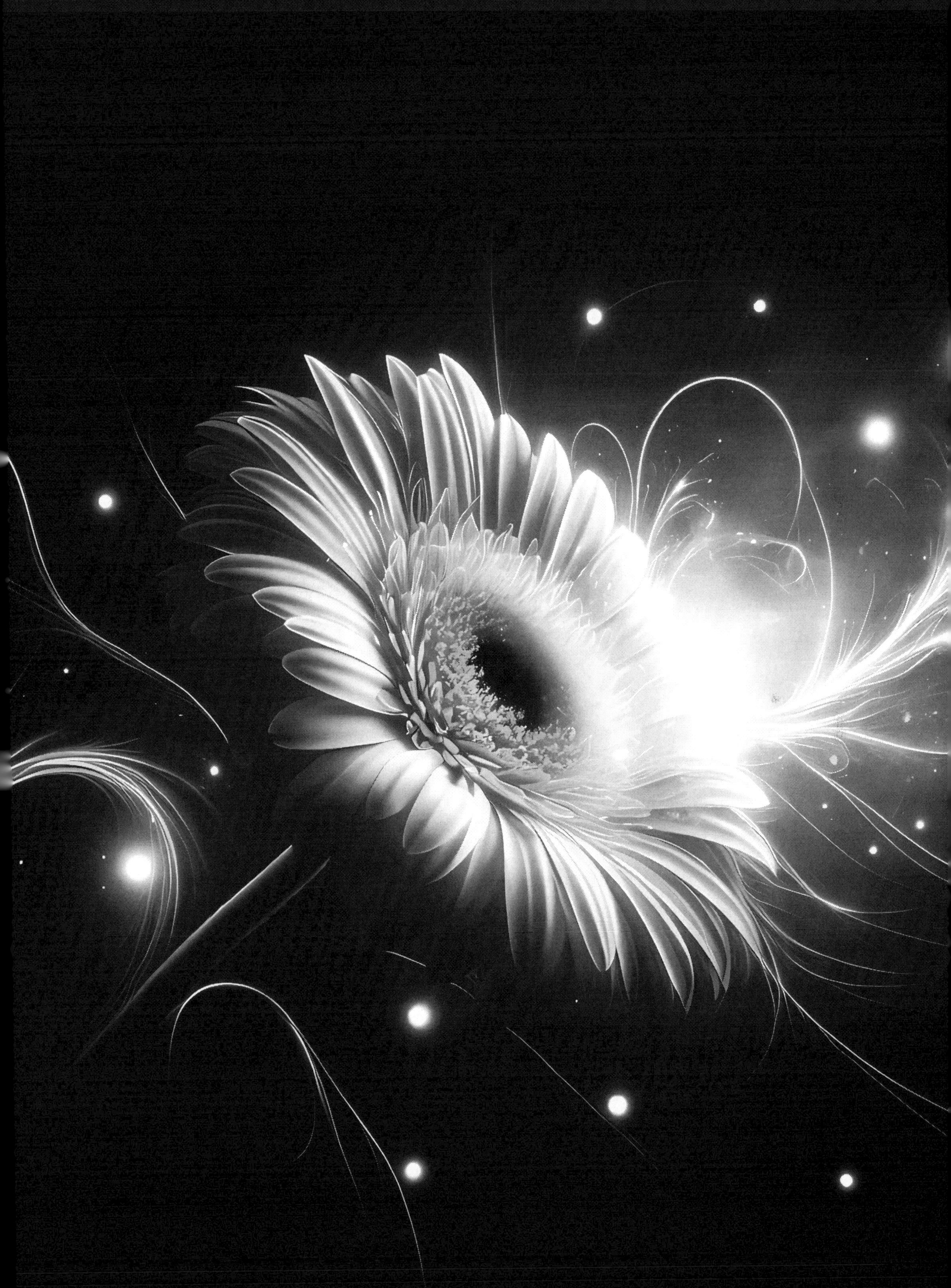

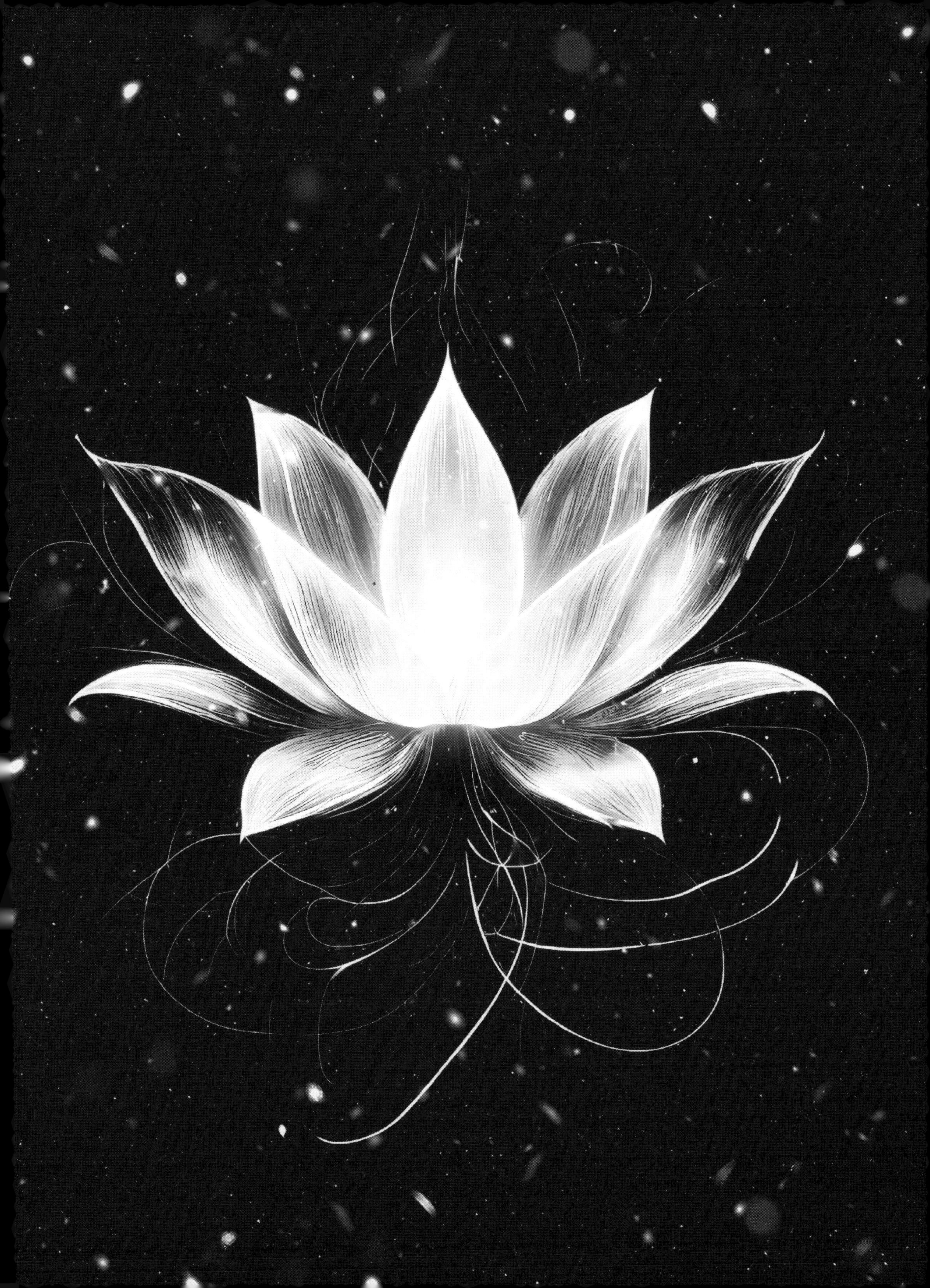

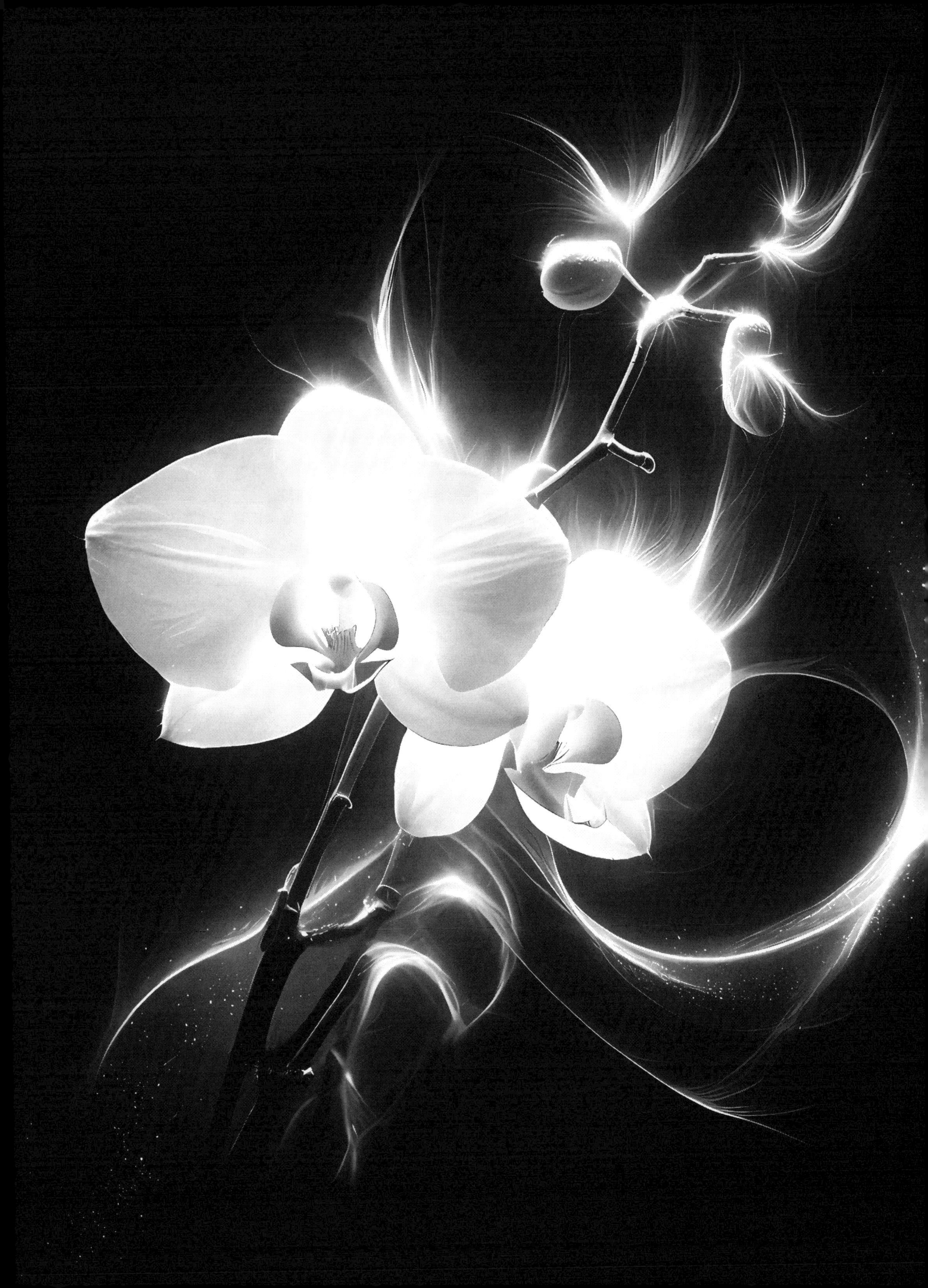

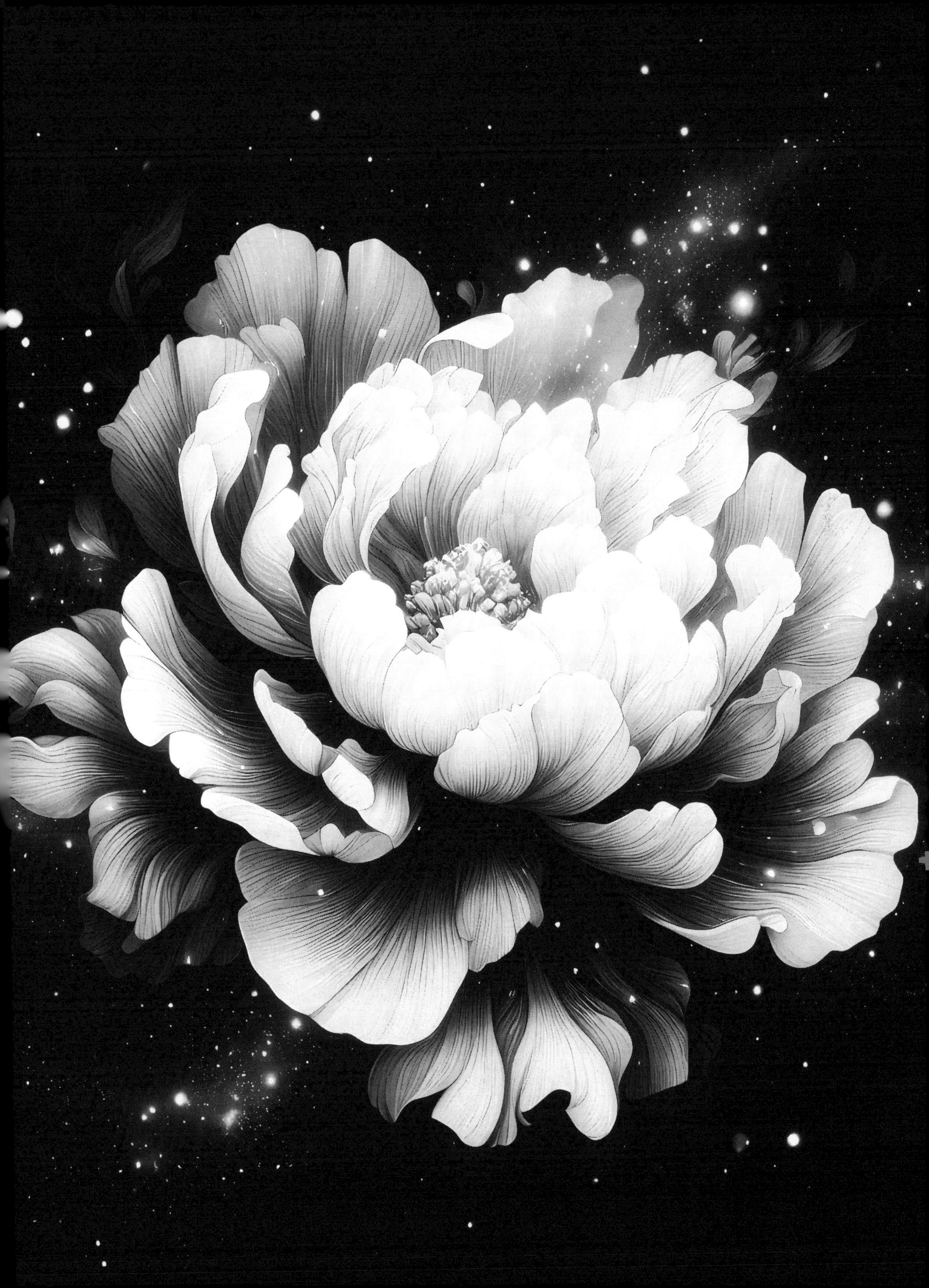

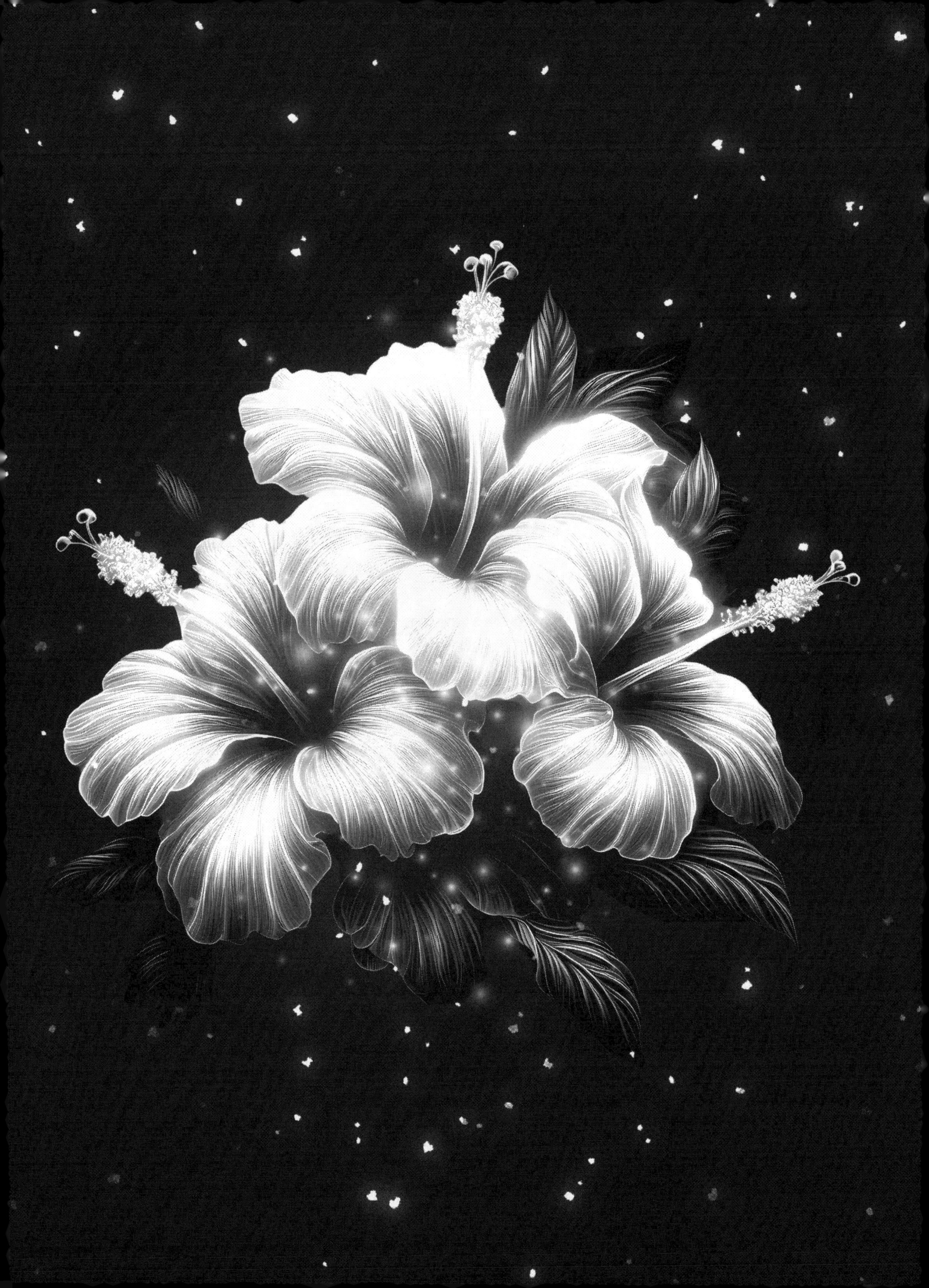

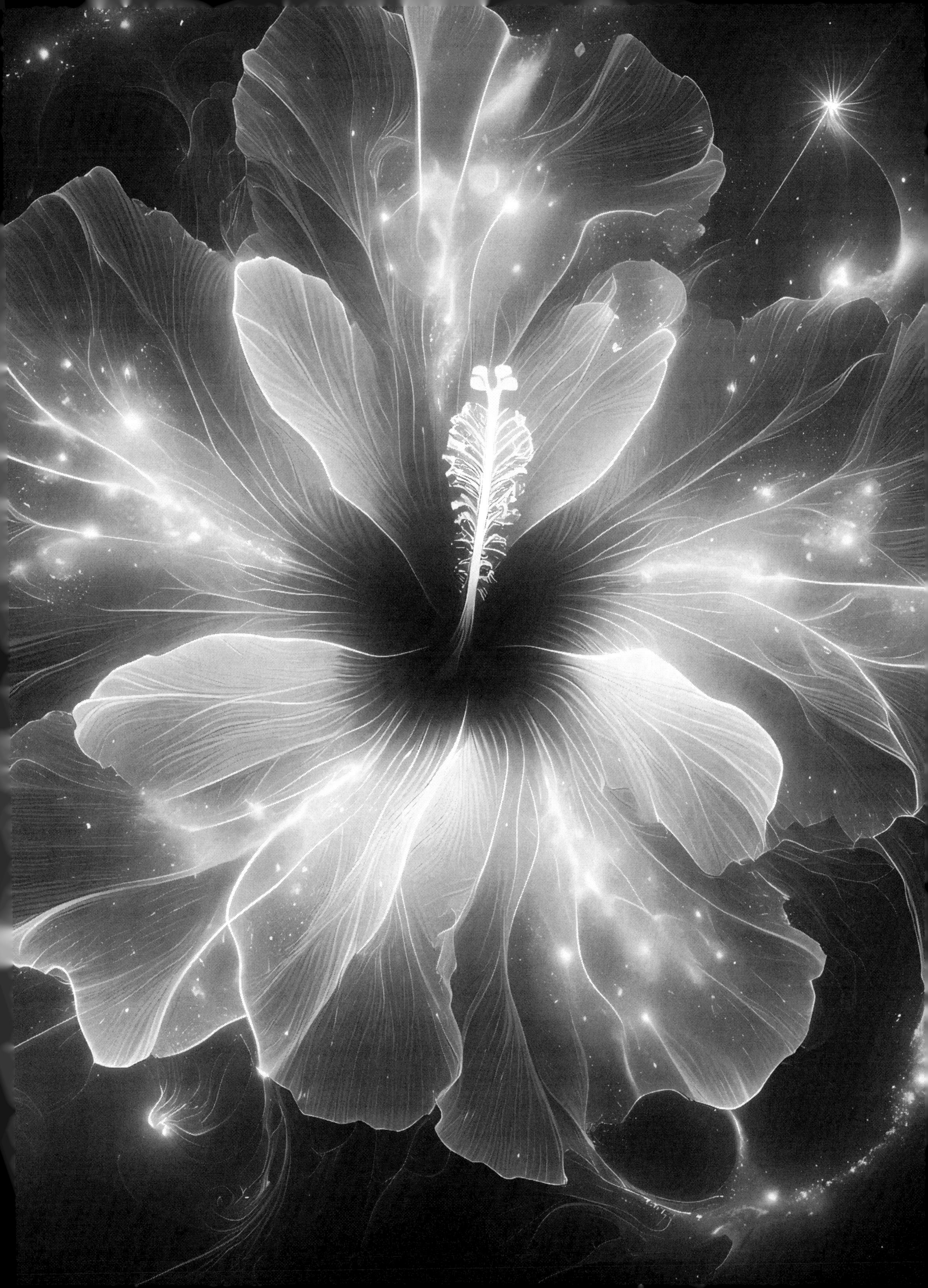

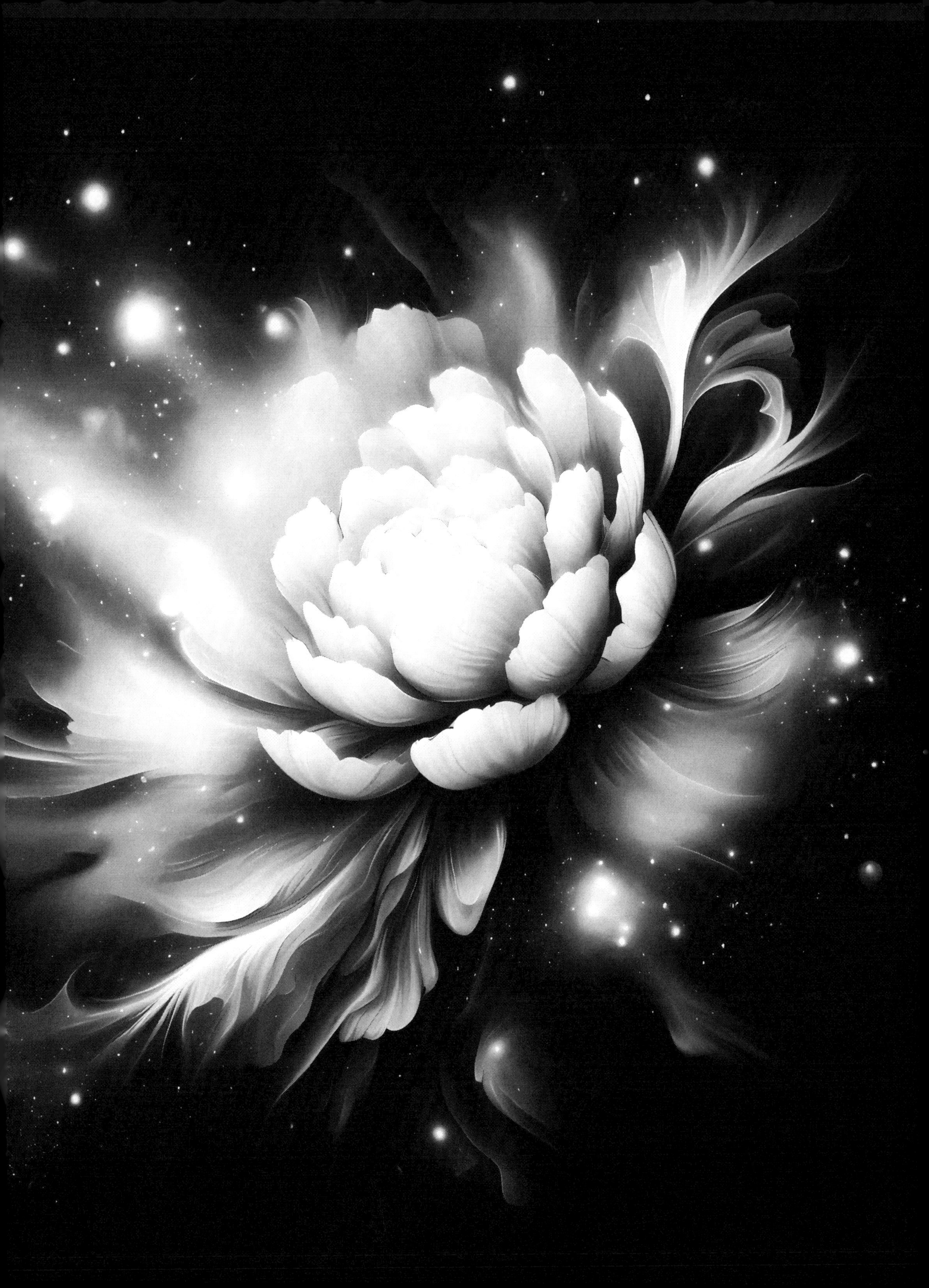

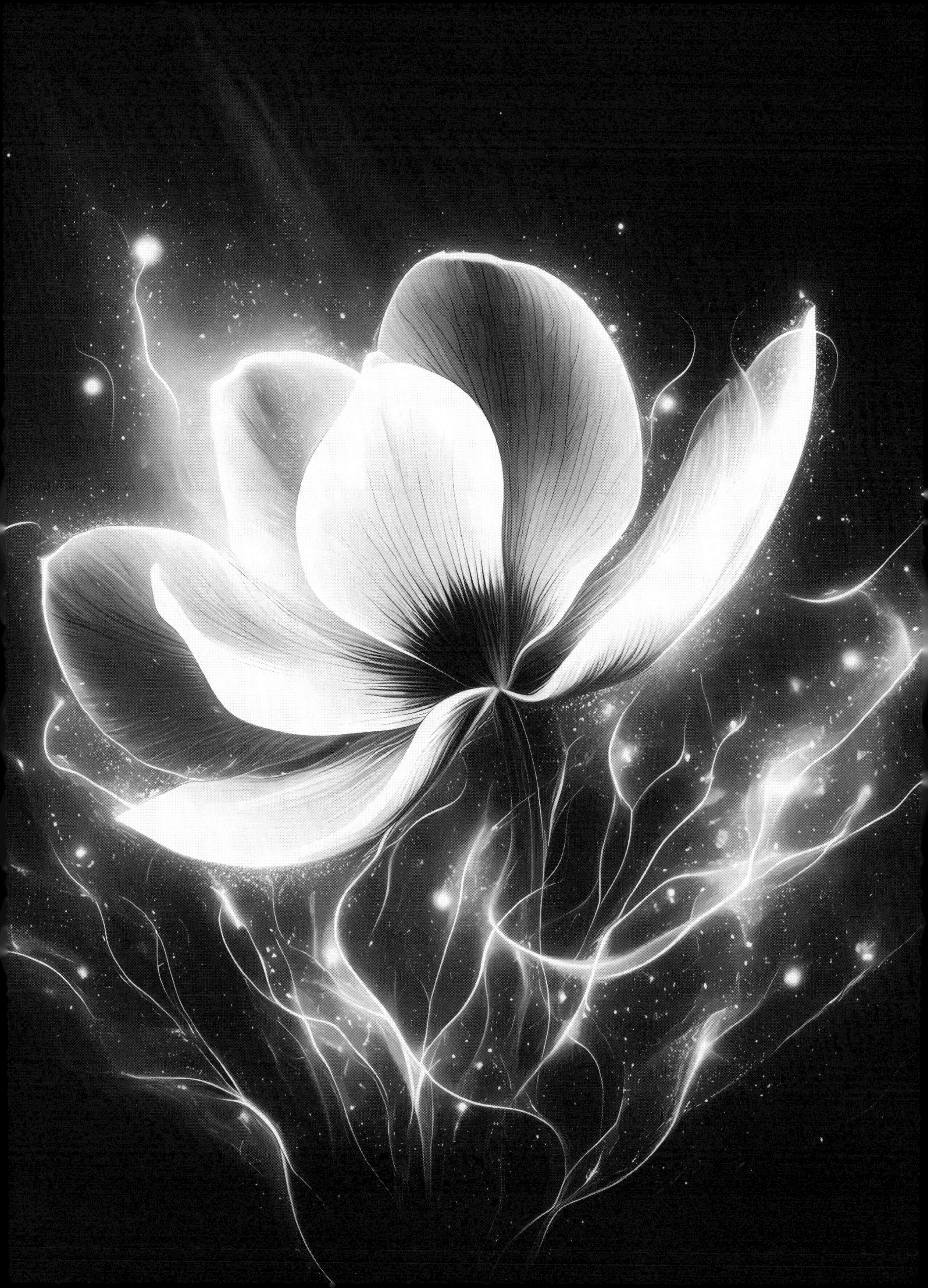

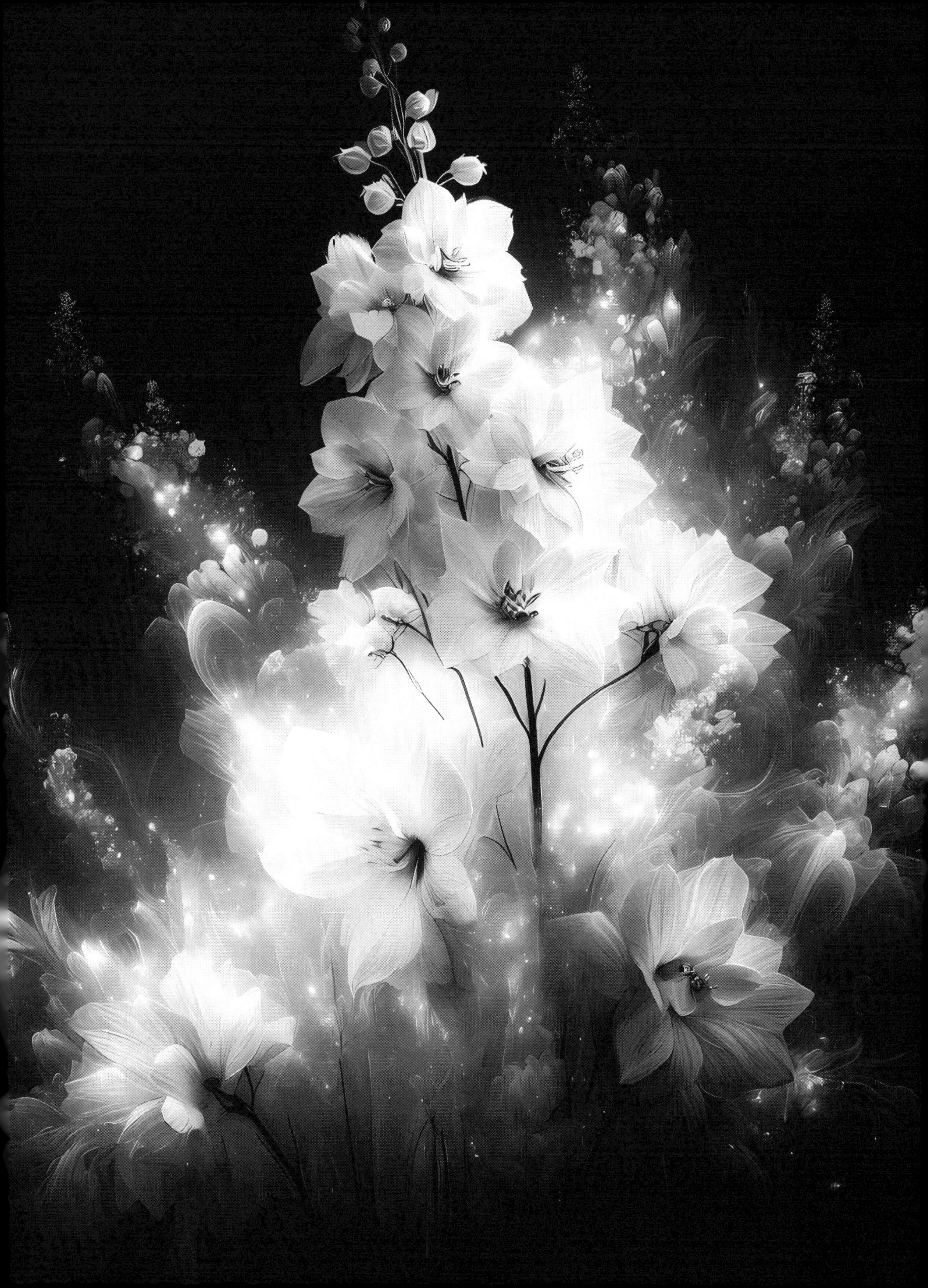

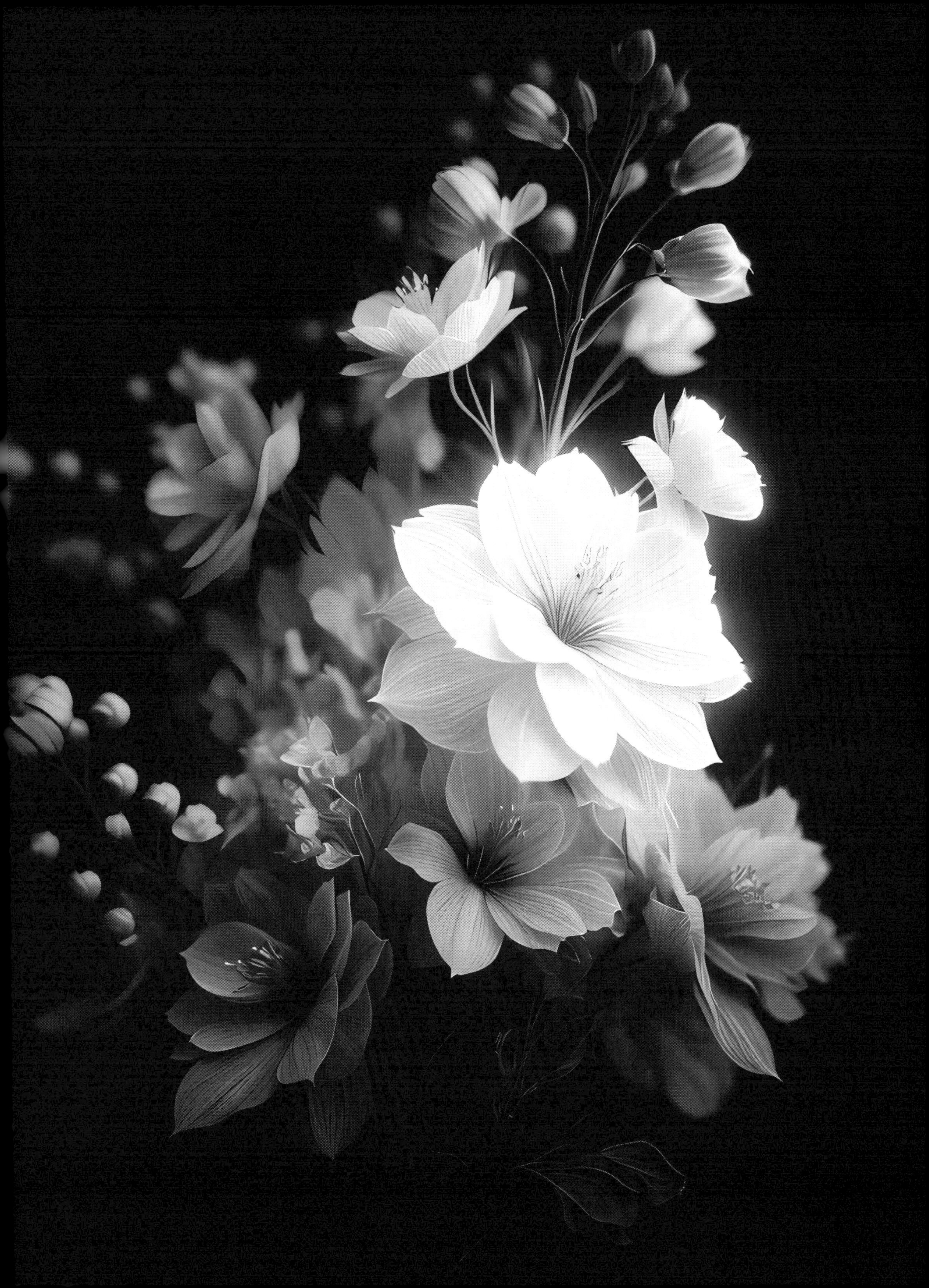

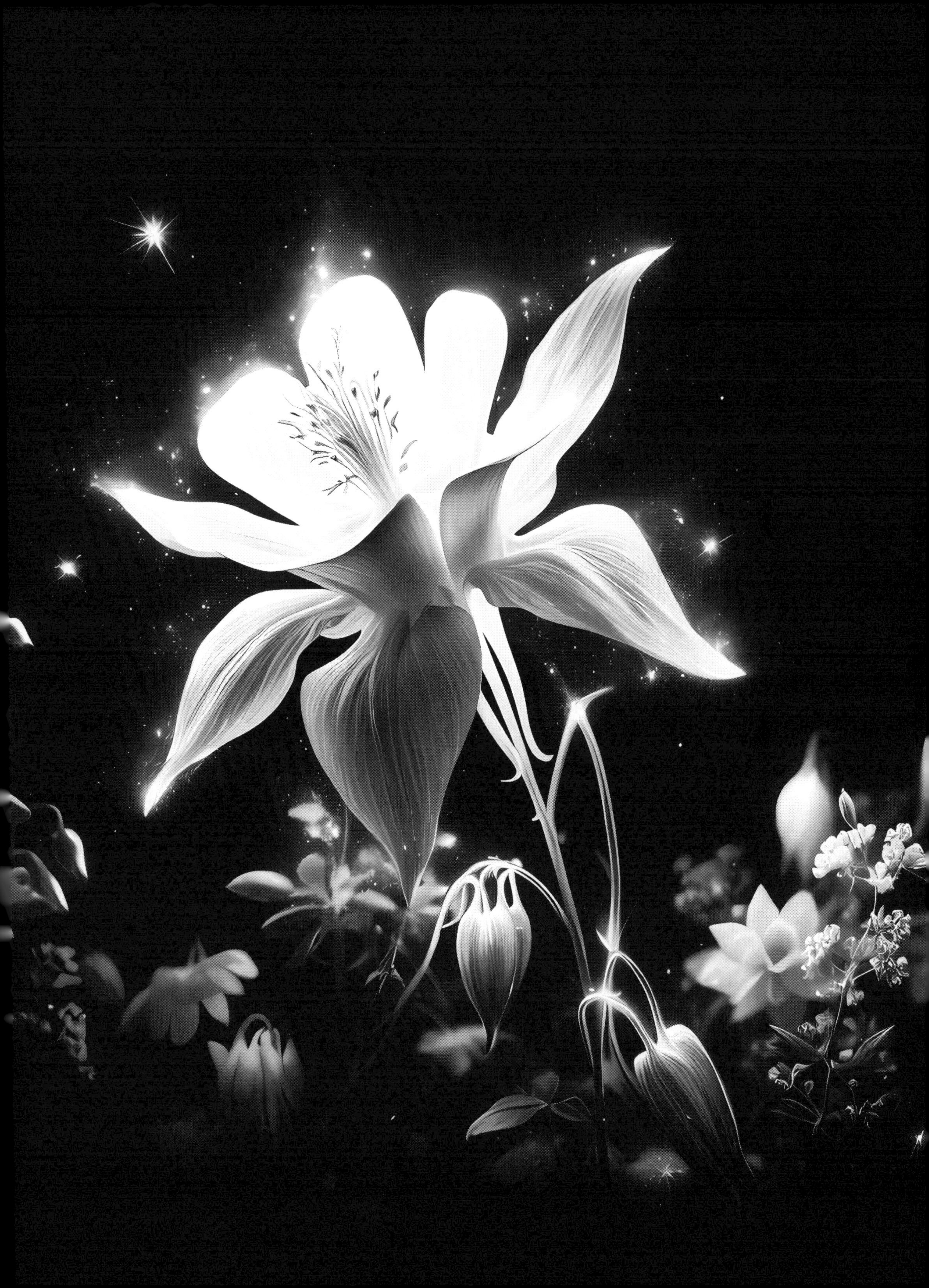

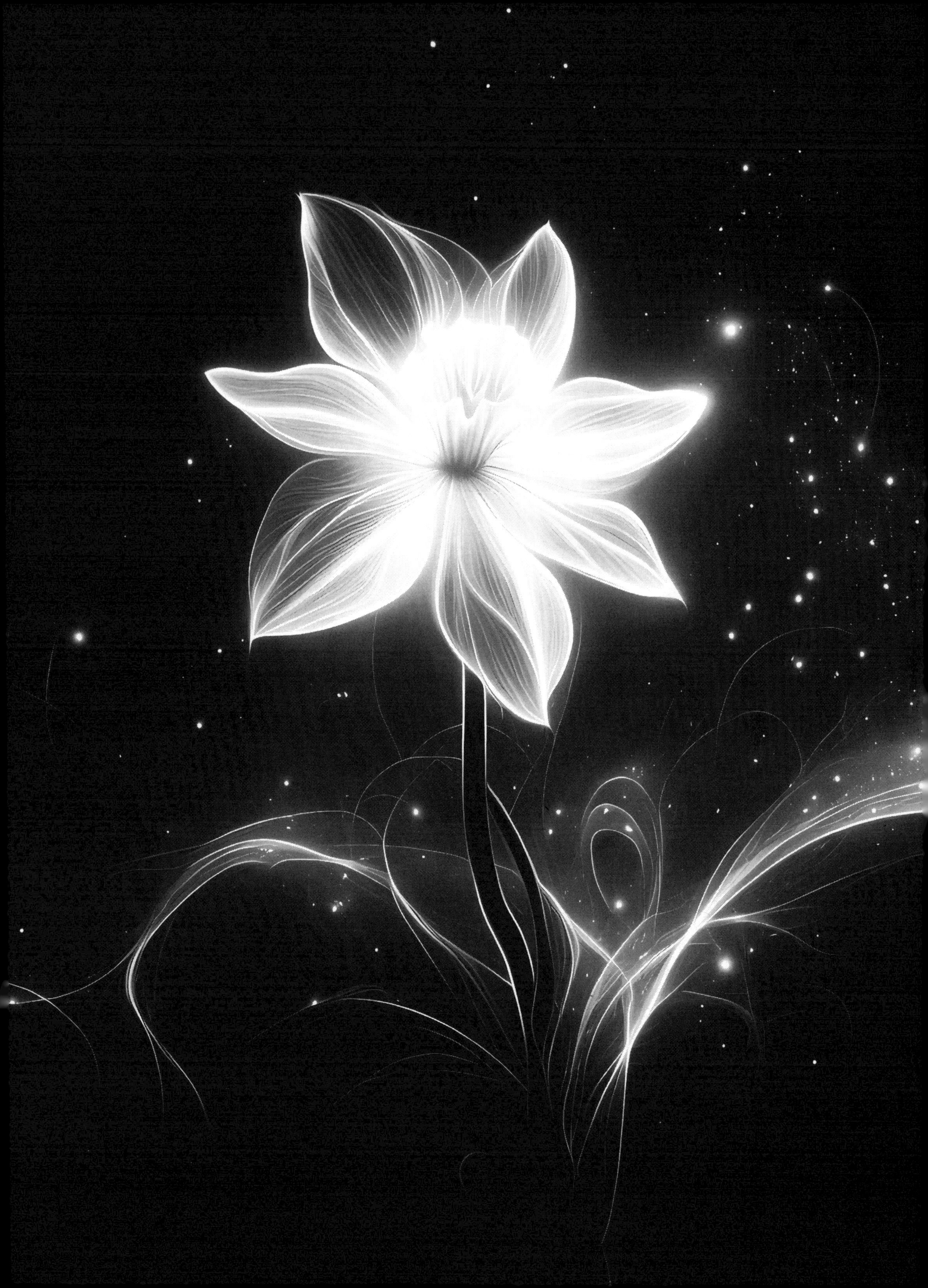

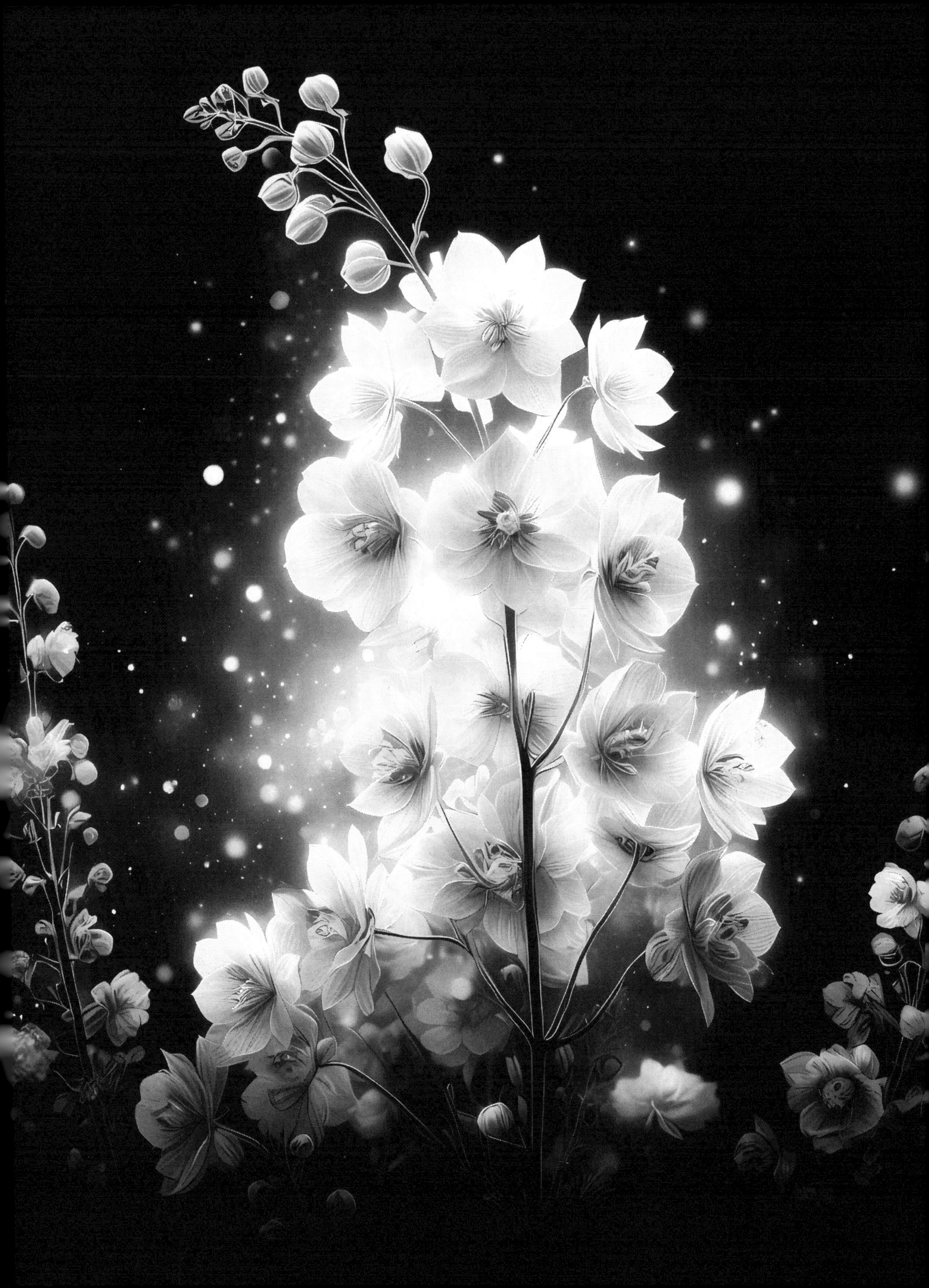

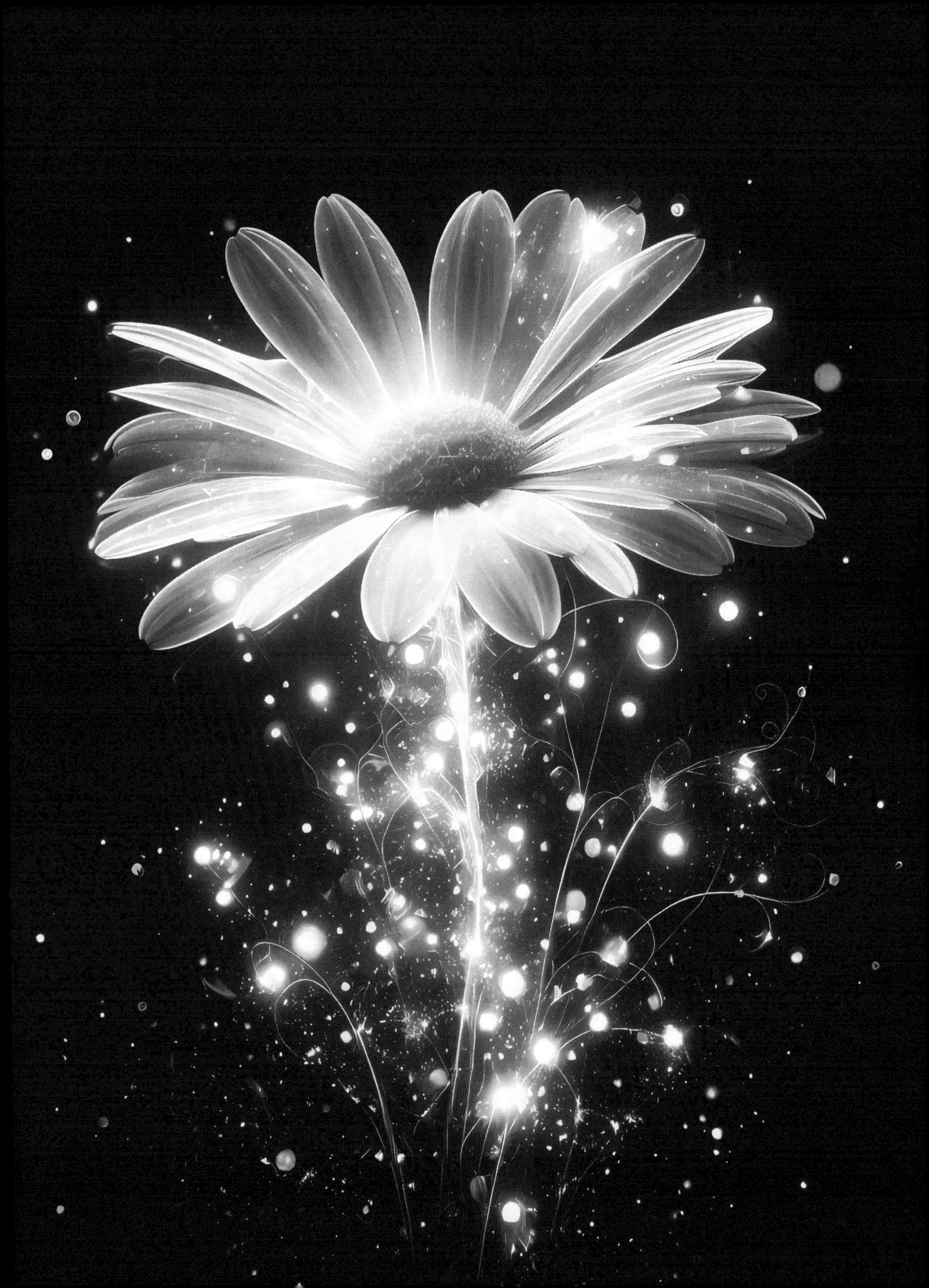

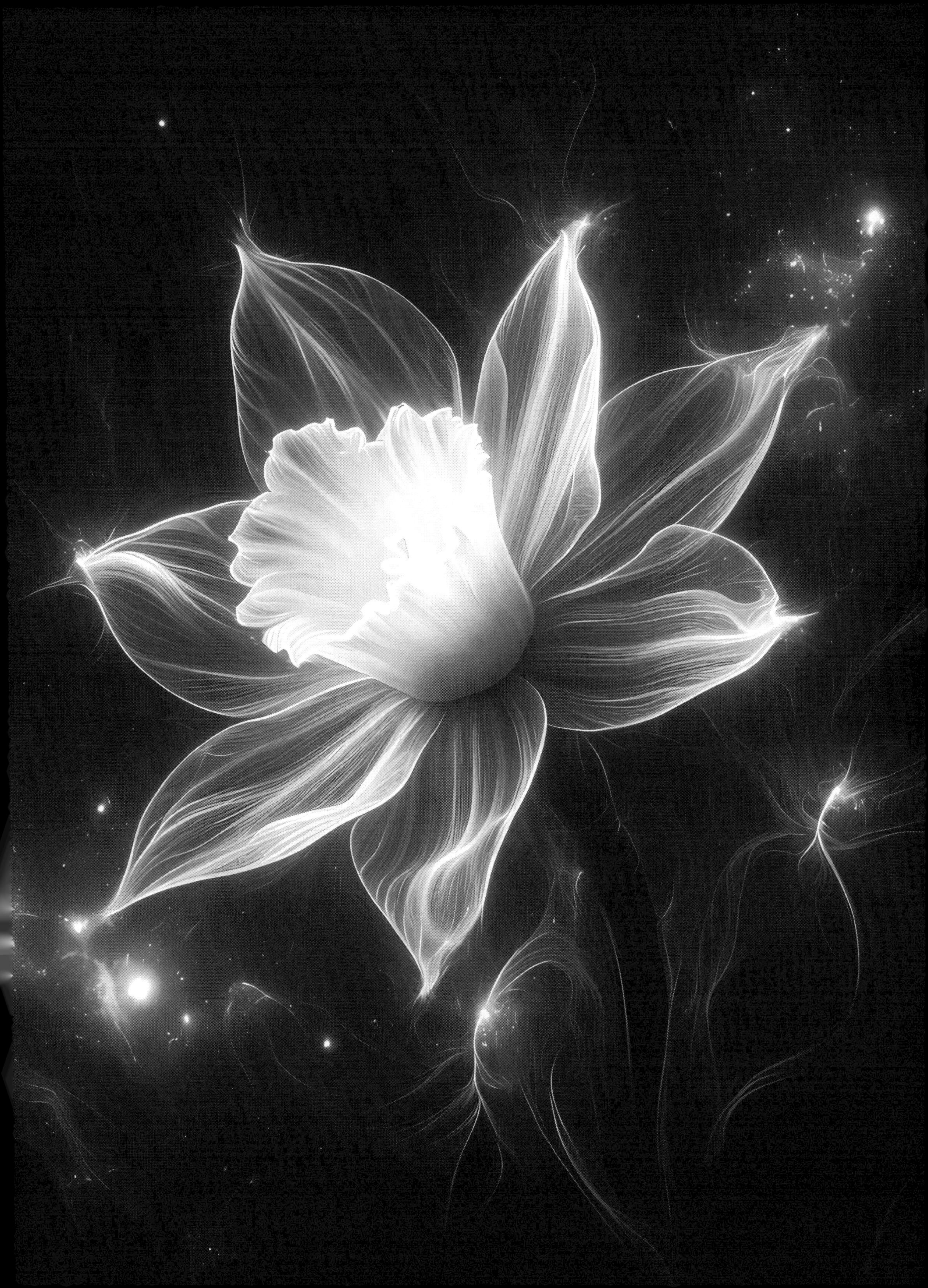

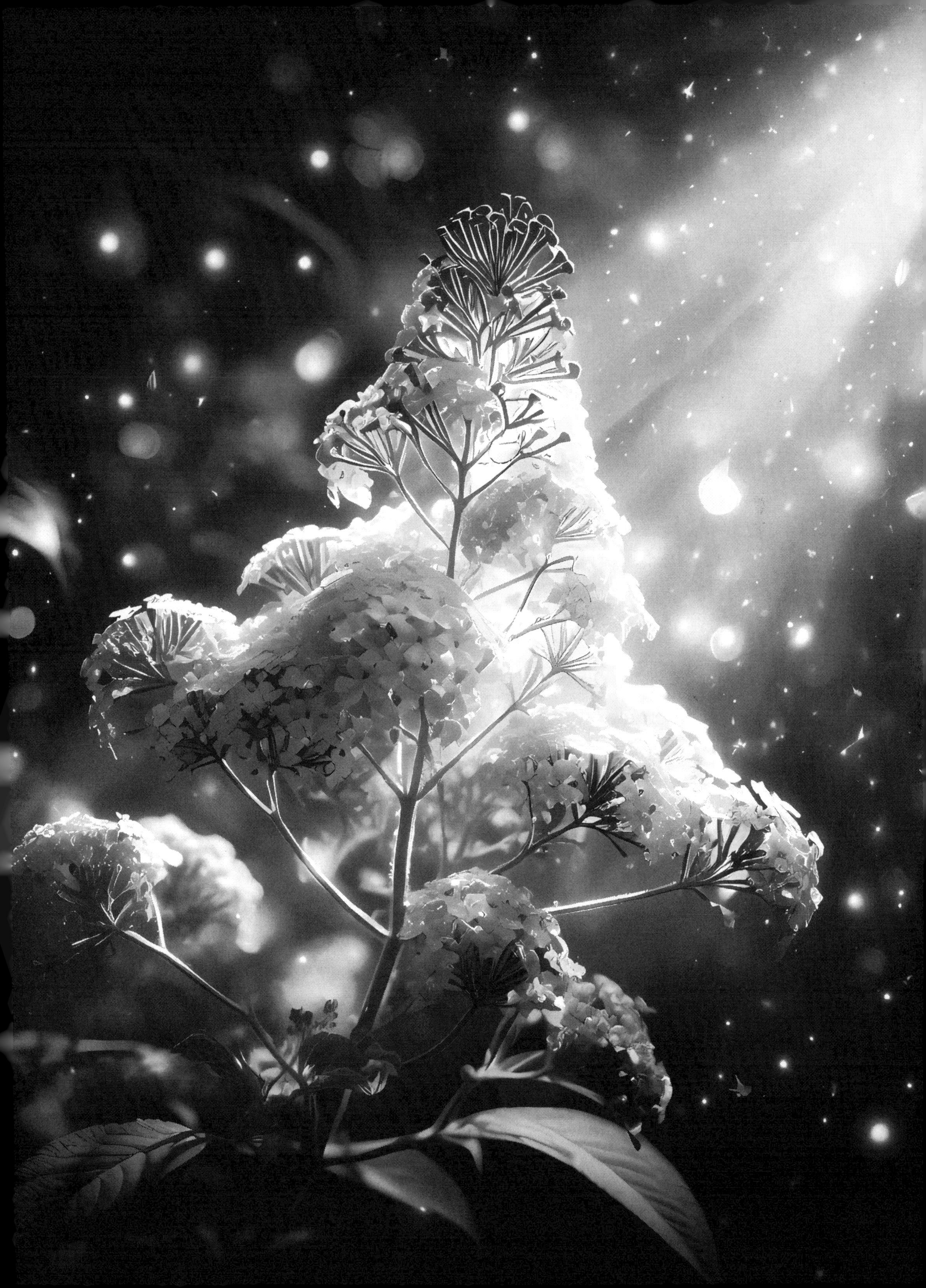

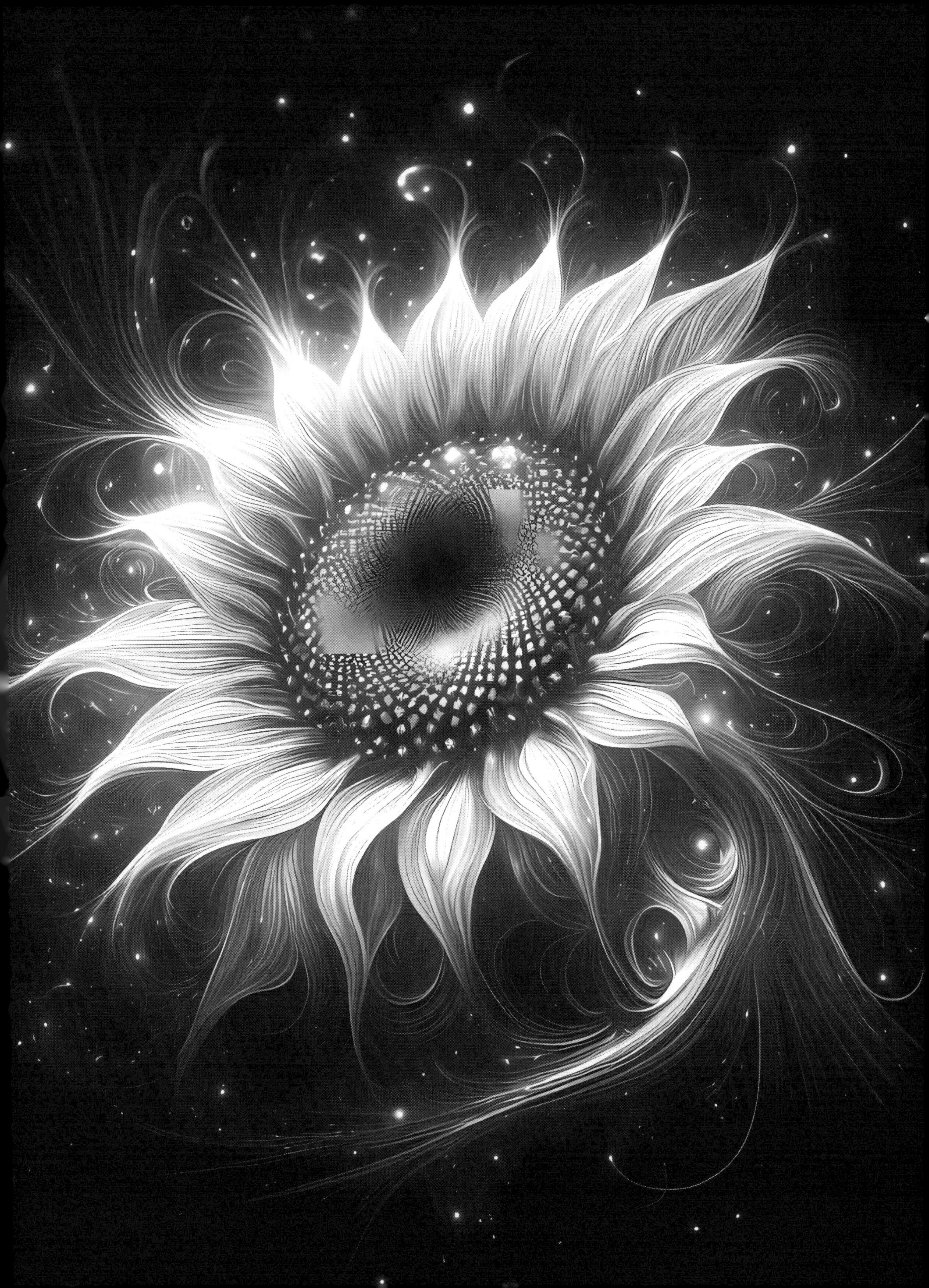

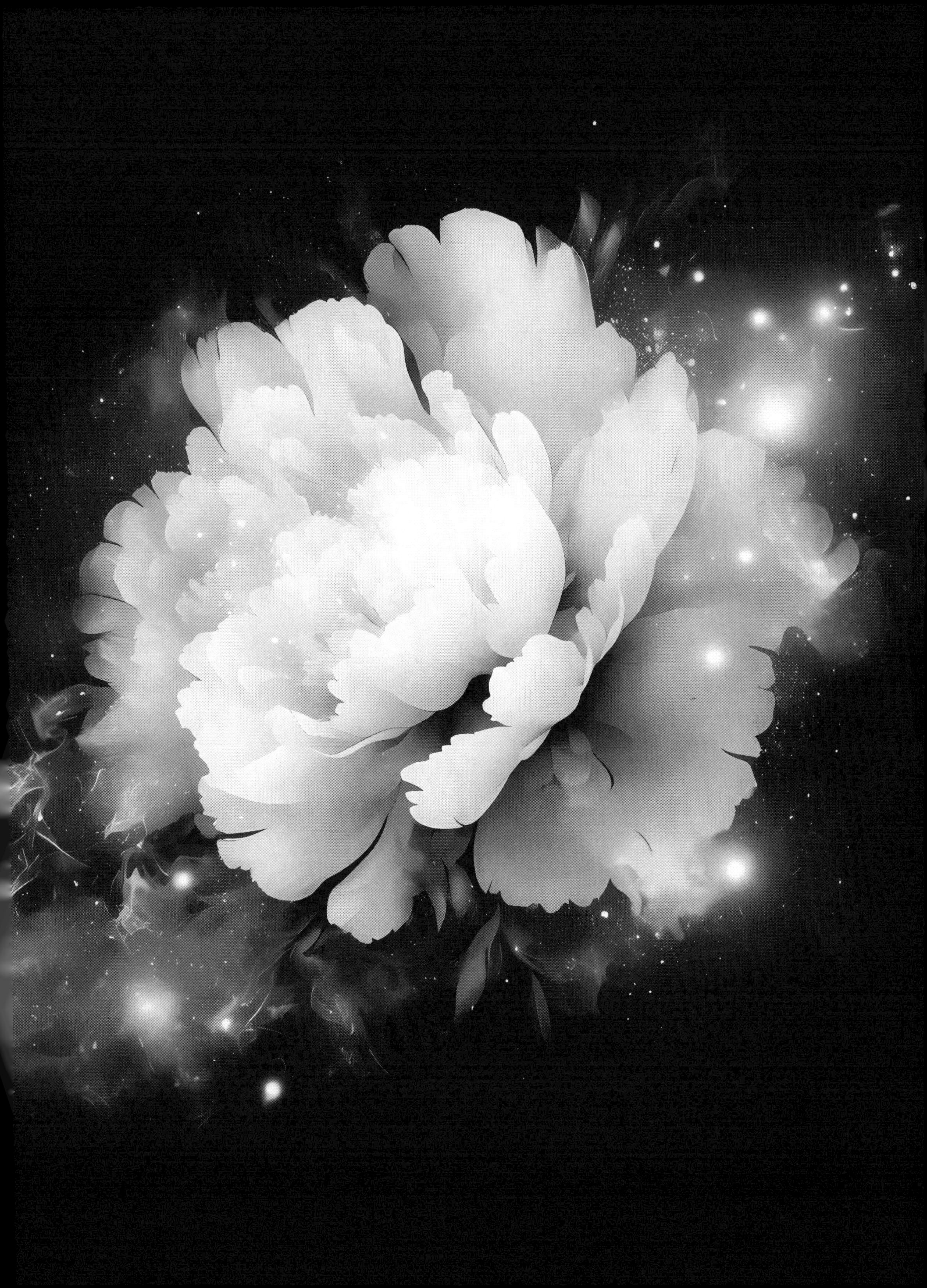

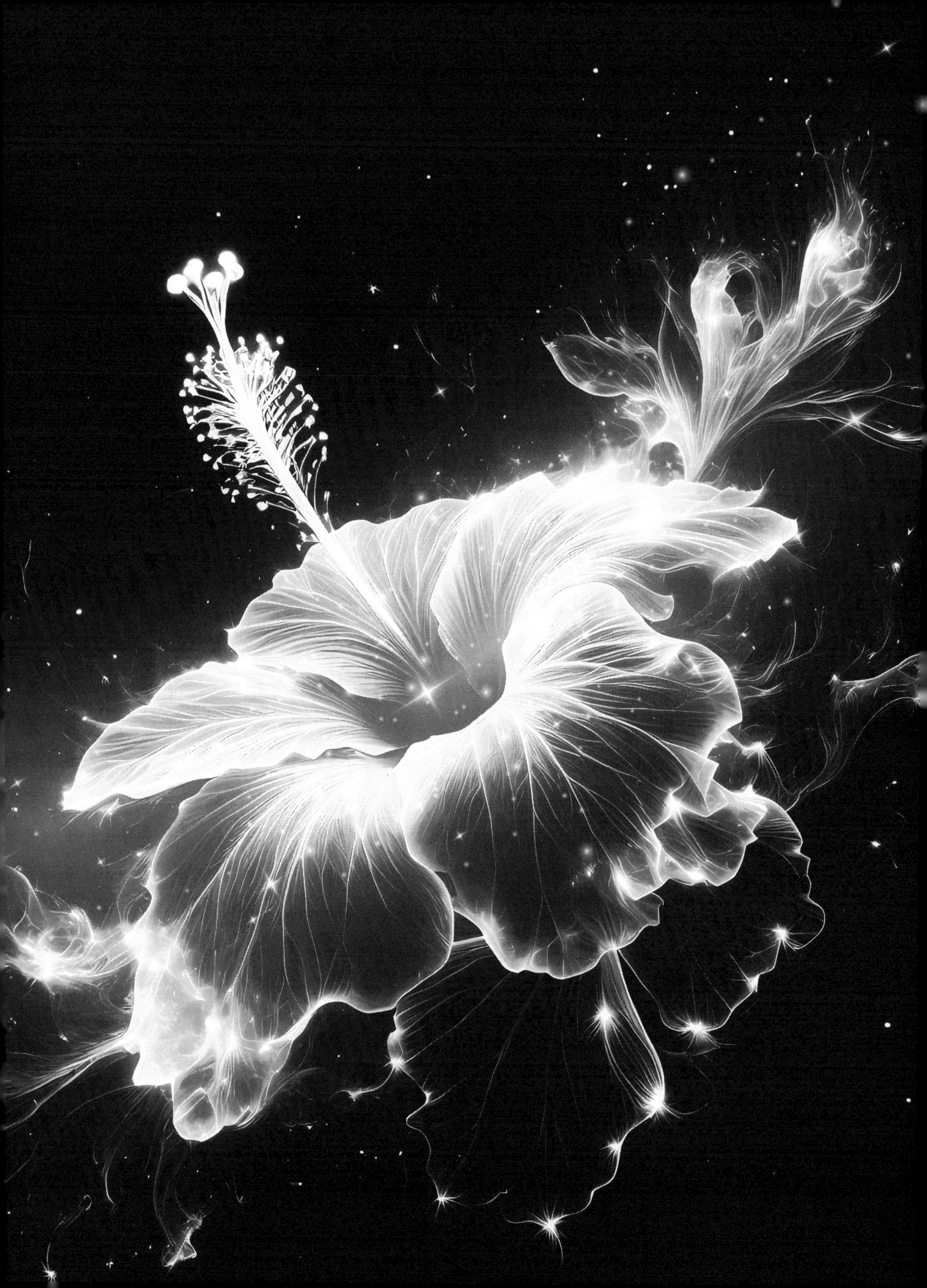

Made in the USA
Las Vegas, NV
29 December 2024

15526688R10057